Frederick J. Turner (signature)

FREDERICK JACKSON TURNER

Wisconsin's Historian of the Frontier

◆

FREDERICK JACKSON TURNER

Wisconsin's Historian of the Frontier

Edited by

M A R T I N   R I D G E

◆

Published by

THE STATE HISTORICAL SOCIETY OF WISCONSIN

MADISON: 1986

For Merle Curti

◆

The State Historical Society of Wisconsin wishes especially to thank Professor George H. Miller of Ripon for his generous contribution to this project, Ms. Patricia Anderson of the Wisconsin Humanities Committee for her encouragement and organizational support, and the National Endowment for the Humanities for additional support.

Library of Congress Cataloging in Publication Data:
Frederick Jackson Turner: Wisconsin's Historian of the Frontier
Contents: Introduction by Martin Ridge / Young Fred Turner by
    Ray Allen Billington / The Significance of the Frontier in
    American History by Frederick Jackson Turner / The Signficance
    of History by Frederick Jackson Turner / Bibliographic Note
    by James P. Danky
1. Turner, Frederick Jackson, 1861–1932.
2. Frontier and Pioneer Life—United States—Historiography.
I. Ridge, Martin, 1923–. II. Billington, Ray Allen, 1903–1981.
III. Turner, Frederick Jackson, 1861–1932.
E175.5.T83F74 1986   973'.072024   86-5996
ISBN 0-87020-246-4

PREFACE

THIS BOOK BEGAN through the efforts of Paul Hass, senior editor at the State Historical Society of Wisconsin, who first approached me to write a brief introduction to a fine print collectors' edition of Frederick Jackson Turner's essay, "The Significance of the Frontier in American History." That edition, published in 1985 by the Silver Buckle Press of the University of Wisconsin–Madison, attracted the attention of the Wisconsin Humanities Committee, which has sponsored this re-publication not only of "The Significance of the Frontier in American History" but also Turner's long-out-of-print essay, "The Significance of History," and Ray Allen Billington's brilliant account of Turner's youth, "Young Fred Turner," which first appeared in the *Wisconsin Magazine of History*.

Taken together, the three essays are a reminder of the powerful influence Wisconsin has had on American historical writing. No one has better than Billington in brief compass captured the sense of the state's cultural landscape after the Civil War. He gives us a picture of Turner's Wisconsin that will ring true to anyone familiar with the state's people and its life. Moreover, he explains how a youth from the "backwoods" with an inquiring mind could become a major figure in our history. Turner's essay on "The Significance of History" indicates the intellectual integrity and imagination that characterized his approach to learning. It is also a vivid and healthy reminder of why the study of history should be a vital part of our educational system. Turner explains what the "New History" of the twentieth century is and how it should be studied if it is to be meaningful. "The Significance of the Frontier in American History" is a seminal work that should be read and reread by people who believe that history has meaning and importance to life. Partly because of its enormous impact and partly because it was the work of a young University of Wisconsin professor it deserves widespread distribution, especially at a time when many Americans have doubts about the nation's values and goals. It remains an important essay for this generation.

I wish to thank Paul Hass and James P. Danky of the State Historical Society for encouraging me to write a new introduction for these essays and the Wisconsin Humanities Committee for making available to the people of Wisconsin this valued part of their heritage.

MARTIN RIDGE

The Huntington Library
San Marino, California

CONTENTS

PHOTOGRAPHS
*illustrative of the life and
career of Frederick Jackson Turner
are selected from the Iconographic
Collections of the State Historical
Society of Wisconsin.*

Introduction

Martin Ridge

◆

THERE IS LITTLE NEED to justify the publication of these several essays by and about Frederick Jackson Turner, Wisconsin's most famous historian. He had a profound impact not only on his own generation of historians but also on subsequent thinkers. He was not the author of many books, but was a brilliant interpretative essayist at a time when many other American historians were doing the rudimentary ground-work in American history by editing documents and writing turgid monographs. He was also a leader in the struggle for the professionaliza-tion of history as a discipline and a rigorous opponent of amateurs. Turner had a profoundly humane view of the role that history could play in the education of the average citizen but a very jealous and compelling one when he argued that without the study of history Americans risked rearing a generation of statesmen without knowledge and a population without a sense of citizenship. He saw in the American frontiering expe-rience a key to understanding our history.[1] A mere listing of books and articles that deal with his ideas fills a volume, and there is little evidence that the study of his work will diminish.[2]

That this collection of essays should begin with one by Ray Allen Billington is entirely appropriate, because he was this century's foremost defender and interpreter of Frederick Jackson Turner as well as his biog-rapher.[3] Billington, like Turner, was Middle Westerner, a graduate of the University of Wisconsin, and a one-time journalist who eventually found history to be his first love. Billington, however, was not an early convert to frontier history. As a graduate student at Harvard, he was more inter-ested in social and intellectual history; and he wrote his dissertation with Arthur Schlesinger, the dean of American cultural and intellectual histori-ans. (Billington did audit a course with Frederick Merk, Turner's loyal disciple, who had succeeded him at both Wisconsin and Harvard.)

1

Billington turned to the study of frontier history when a good friend, James Blaine Hedges, asked him to co-author a textbook on the subject. The book was not designed to be based on original research in the sources but it was to be deeply rooted in Turner's idea of the frontier and was to incorporate the material in the most recently published scholarly books and articles on the subject. Hedges virtually dropped out of the project, completing only three chapters of the book, and Billington became increasingly immersed in writing *the* book that Turner would have written had he been the kind of historian who wrote books rather than essays.[4]

From this introduction to frontier history, Billington moved to a study of Turner's personal papers in the Huntington Library in San Marino, California; and there, reading Turner's letters, unpublished essays, lectures, and notes, he fell under Turner's spell and began a search for the sources of his ideas.[5] It was a golden opportunity for a scholar interested in American intellectual history and culture, partly because Turner played an integral role in shaping American historical thought and partly because Turner was interested in what made American society distinctive. Eventually Billington, like Turner himself, was destined to seek the meaning of the frontier in American life rather than to write monographic studies about the frontiering experience of the American people.[6]

Despite the large number of books and articles that argued Turner was not an original thinker and his ideas could be traced to the research and writings of other scholars, including the Italian political economist Archille Loria, Billington believed that Turner could not have evolved his ideas had he not been reared on the edge of the frontier. It was not that his parents came from old-line New England Puritan stock or that his family had been part of a westering contingent that wandered into Wisconsin to make a new life; rather it was living in Portage, Wisconsin, after the Civil War that made him aware of the differences between frontier folk and activities and the people and practices of the American East and Europe.

Although Portage was no longer a frontier community but a bustling town of somewhat less than 5,000 souls when Turner was growing to manhood, the accounts of Indians, fur traders, trappers, and Irish lumbermen that made up the early history of the place still echoed in the streets. And Turner himself could recollect from his boyhood seeing Indians being shipped off to reservations, loggers tying up their rafts, and a dead man—the victim of a lynch mob—left hanging as an example. To live in Portage during these years was for Turner to feel a part of the great surge of national energy that was subduing, taming, and developing the country, as well as Americanizing immigrants. All of this Billington brilliantly tells in his essay "Young Fred Turner," ending his narrative and analysis with episodes that embrace Turner's life before he went to college. After reading Billington's narrative, one is convinced that whatever Turner learned from books and manuscripts only confirmed what he absorbed from his personal experience with the people of Portage and from the brooks, lakes, and the piney landscape of Wisconsin.

The University of Wisconsin was on the threshold of greatness in 1880 when Turner arrived in Madison. He made the most of the opportunities the school offered, reveling in the life of a social fraternity, editing the school paper, engaging in the debates and exercises of literary societies, and capturing the prestigious Burrows Prize, the most coveted oratorical award the university could bestow. Meanwhile he soaked up the knowledge that the conventional curriculum offered undergraduates. Although he read widely in classical literature and became an expert rhetorician, his first love was history; and he was befriended and deeply influenced by Professor William Francis Allen, a Harvard-educated and German-trained scholar of ancient and medieval history who occupied the university's history professorship.

On graduation in 1884 Turner first turned to a career in journalism. He worked briefly for the *Milwaukee Sentinel,* the *Chicago Inter-Ocean,* and the *Wisconsin State Register.* His reporting was accurate, his style clear and terse; but the opportunity to return to the university to teach history overcame his promise of success as a newspaperman. This was not an easy decision for Turner to make because professorial posts in history were very few in 1885. Gaining one required substantial advanced education and demonstrable evidence of skill as a lecturer.

Nevertheless, Turner accepted a post in the history department, filling in for Professor Allen, who was on leave. He remained at Wisconsin to work for a master of arts degree, which he received in 1888. His thesis subject, "The Influence of the Fur Trade in the Development of Wisconsin," was as close to his heart and personal experience as it was to the original documents and manuscripts in the State Historical Society of Wisconsin on which it was based, for the Society had already acquired a distinguished collection of Western Americana.

To become a professional historian Turner needed a Ph.D., and he decided to attend The Johns Hopkins University in Baltimore. At that time Hopkins was the premier institution in the nation for graduate work, with a faculty that listed such noteworthy social scientists as Albion Small, Richard T. Ely, Woodrow Wilson, J. Franklin Jameson, and Herbert Baxter Adams. Turner soon earned the respect and lasting friendship of these men. Time would prove that Turner's contemporaries in the graduate program—such as Charles Homer Haskins who became a distinguished professor of medieval history at Harvard—would be as renowned as their teachers.

The history students and the faculty at Hopkins carried on their work with the fervor of religious zealots. They wanted not only to make the study and teaching of history into a profession but also to create a new discipline of history that was based on a larger knowledge and a more rigorous method of research. Moreover, they were well aware of the works of the best European scholars and of the few Americans who were writing with critical skill. These men were their models, and the students sought to emulate them. Turner thrived in this atmosphere, where no assumption was sacred and ideas were shared, discussed, and openly criticized.

Yet even the Johns Hopkins history department was not entirely free of doctrine. Herbert Baxter Adams dominated it, and he propounded the "germ theory," which explained historical development in terms of "germs" or antecedents. According to Adams, all American institutions found their origin in medieval Teutonic tribal structures. He saw little utility to studying American institutional history *per se*. Adams' thinking was entirely compatible with the ideas of the leading literary scholars of the era, who were busy establishing the critical linkages in Anglo-Saxon and American literature, but was virtually sterile to historians deeply interested in the American past because it denied the possibility that anything original or unique could stem from the American experience. When Turner wrote his doctoral dissertation, which was an elaboration and expansion of his master's thesis, he incorporated Adams' views by including a discussion of the fur trade in the ancient world, although he showed that the Wisconsin experience was essentially different.

Turner rejoined the faculty of the University of Wisconsin in 1889, where the premature death of William Francis Allen opened the way for his promotion to a professorship. He carried with him to Wisconsin the zeal, skills, and goals that he had acquired at Hopkins, and he immediately won a strong following among the better students. Anything but a narrow academic, Turner brought to his work a remarkable knowledge of European history and of the research developments in the cognate disciplines of economics, sociology, geography, and politics. He shared with his faculty colleagues in their desire to make the university the state's palladium, but he was also determined to make the discipline of history central to the university because he believed sincerely that the study of history could contribute to improving the lives of the people of Wisconsin.

An opportunity to present an address to the Southwestern Wisconsin

Teachers' Association gave Turner a platform from which to explain why he felt that history was important to the people of the state as well as what it was and how it should be studied in a free society. The circumstances surrounding the writing of the address and its delivery are unknown. In fact, it may never have been given; but a version was published in the *Wisconsin Journal of Education* in 1891. Considering Turner's age and status in the historical profession, his essay is a remarkable document. Had the essay been prepared by an historian of national prominence, it would have been heralded as an eloquent and pathbreaking article marking the new direction the discipline of history was to follow for generations to come. It remains today a statement from which few if any historians would dissent. "The Significance of History" may have been "buried" in a minor Wisconsin educational magazine for almost half a century (it was published by the University of Wisconsin Press in 1938 as part of *The Early Writing of Frederick Jackson Turner*), but its ideas and analysis undergirded what was taught as the New History by the nation's great historians of Turner's generation.

Turner's "The Significance of History" was more his personal statement to teachers of history than a focused essay, for he touched on a variety of subjects. If it has a thesis, it is that history is neither a mindless chronicle of the past nor an interesting literary pageant written to enchant rather than necessarily inform readers. History is "all the remains that have come down to us from the past, studied with all the critical and interpretive power that the present can bring to the task."

Turner was as critical of authors who sacrificed truth to drama and who held history to be a branch of literature as he was of historians who believed that it was simply past politics and the activities of powerful elite groups. The lives of common people were important and historians should not overlook the doings of the "degraded tillers of the soil." History was tragedy as well as progress. The only way to study the whole past was to recognize the work of other scholars, especially economists, geographers, political scientists, and theologians, because their insights could illuminate the past in productive ways. Nor would Turner ignore artifacts, myths, folklore, or tradition, because explanation required as complete an examination of sources as possible.

Turner was also concerned with the kind of truths that history told. Even the most meticulous use of scientific methods could not overcome factors that prevented historians from ever producing an "ultimate" history. Historians were bound by their culture, values, experience, and context. Herodotus, Thucydides, Livy, Hume, and Carlyle, Turner warned, were great historians—but they were advocates and partisans of political parties and methods of research that made them creatures of their times. Turner recognized the relativist nature of historical writing and cautioned against orthodoxies. In a way this led him to recapitulate the position of his mentor, Herbert Baxter Adams, because he stressed the importance of continuity and the unity of the past. National history that ignored world history was little better than tribal history and shared its dangerous implications for conflict rather than world understanding.

Turner pointed to the fact that some of Europe's great historians were also its leading statesmen. The United States could make not such a boast, and the results were evident in the quality of their debates and understanding of world problems. It was imperative for the future of the nation that the general public and policy makers escape from parochialism so the United States could act wisely in a world increasingly integrated politically and economically. Only the study of history could contribute substantially to the creation of that sense of citizenship so vital to development of the nation. It was the history teacher and the public library that held the key to our nation's future.

The publication of "The Significance of History" indicates that Turner was entering the most creative period of his life. He had at his fingertips the resources of the State Historical Society of Wisconsin, and as Wisconsin emerged as a great public university he was in the company of one of the most innovative faculties of his day. It is fascinating to determine what books he read, with whom he talked about his work, and what periodicals he clipped and underscored. It is also possible to trace the evolution of much of his thought through his published and unpublished essays and speeches. There is no mystery about what was common knowledge—what "ideas were in the air"—when Turner began teaching and writing. But no one has yet proved, nor did Turner himself adequately explain precisely when, but more especially how, his reading and ideas coalesced into the essay he was to present at the Historical Congress in Chicago at the World's Columbian Exposition of 1893. In it, Turner would demonstrate a renewed interest in a much narrower view of American history.[7]

It is ironic that Herbert Baxter Adams, whose "germ theory" Turner was to attack, recommended that he participate in the Chicago meeting. At first Turner declined—suggesting instead that one of his students go in his place—but he finally consented to prepare a paper based on his research. He was still working on the address the day it was to be given. After four speakers had tested the audience's mettle by presenting deadeningly old-fashioned scholarly exercises, Turner offered a paper that seemed to pass as unnoticed as the others. But there was a difference. Wisconsin's Turner had issued a manifesto; he proposed an explanation not only of the American past but also of the American character that would stir controversy among historians from that day to this, compel the rewriting of American history textbooks, and profoundly influence the way Americans thought about this nation's past and its future.

Little did Herbert Baxter Adams, or for that matter anyone in the audience, guess that Turner had perceived from his research and thinking a hypothesis—a new key—that would make him the leading American historian of his generation. Although the audience that listened to Turner and the first group of scholars who read the essay were not especially impressed, before the decade had passed the "germ theory" had been superseded. For it, Turner substituted a theory based on the impact of the frontier experience on institutional development. Turner transformed the study of American history from a quest for the Teutonic origins of institutions, a subset of European expansion, into a distinct, independent, and important field of research that had something to say to scholars in other areas of history as well as to researchers in other disciplines.[8]

What is clear is that Turner's genius lay in what psychologists have called divergent thinking. He belonged to a group of highly creative and conceptually advanced protagonists of American history who virtually revolutionized the study of history in this country. It would be unfair to his talent and insight to say that it was inevitable that someone would have challenged the existing schema for studying American history, because the time had come for a "paradigmatic shift," since the hold of conventional ideas, such as Herbert Baxter Adams,' were weakening. Turner did more than stumble forward into the future; his was a bold and dramatic break with the past that by its literary charm and excitement bewitched the generations that were to follow him.

Turner entitled his talk "The Significance of the Frontier in American History." He began by pointing out that the United States Bureau of the Census Report for 1890 had called attention to the fact that for the first time in one hundred years the nation no longer possessed a distinct boundary or frontier line between settled and unsettled portions of the West. Unlike other readers of the report, Turner asked the big question: What did the passing of the frontier mean? In phrasing poetic, prophetic, and provocative he elegantly set forth what came to be called the "Turner thesis"—the frontier experience of the American people had been *a* determining factor in the nation's history and in the making of its national character. The availability of an "area of free land. . . ," he argued, "and the advance of . . . settlement westward explain American development." America's special character stemmed from the fact that its people had to confront "the changes involved in crossing a continent, in winning a wilderness, and in developing at each area of this progress, out of the primitive economic and political conditions of the frontier into the complexity of city life."

The frontier, as Turner described it, was the "meeting point between savagery and civilization," the site of the most rapid and effective Americanization of the population. He argued too that the critical function of the frontier was the promotion of democracy in America. This democracy, a unique variety, was born of access by individuals to free land, which served to formulate a basis for a more egalitarian society, where opportunity to begin again existed for people who had not succeeded in the East and who were now willing to pit themselves against the forces of nature.

For Turner, the westward-moving frontier was the source of American exceptionalism: it was what made America and Americans different from Europe and Europeans. The striking characteristics of Americans—many of them unpleasant—Turner attributed to the needs of a society always in motion, in the process of rebirth and reconstruction as settlers pushed westward and established new communities. Pioneers were often forced to shed their cultural baggage when they encountered the wilderness; the re-creation of institutions in the West was the essence of the process of western settlement. Americans living in a society that had reacted to the impact of a frontier for three hundred years, he argued, were "strong in selfishness and individualism, intolerant of administrative experience and education," and likely to press for individual liberty beyond proper bounds. Frontier democracy was often guilty of anti-social behavior, dubious ethics, and questionable economic and political policy. The personal traits of Americans—coarseness and strength combined with inquisitiveness and acquisitiveness, a lack of interest in esthetics and an emphasis on the pragmatic, a restless unrestrained individualism, and an unquenchable optimism—could all be traced, Turner asserted, to the environmental impact of the frontier.

Turner's America in the late 1890's was the apotheosis of the westering experience. It represented the end product of a triumphal march of trappers, traders, ranchers, miners, loggers, farmers, missionaries, cotton planters, soldiers, and entrepreneurs from a cluster of New England towns and tidewater plantations across the continent. For Turner, the Americans of his day, like the frontier settlers he visualized as conquering a continent, had a blind eye for hard truths and a clear one for great expectations.

Little wonder that the public at large and the historical profession embraced Turner's perception of American history. It provided a usable past for a people who were increasingly aware of their emerging role in world leadership and equally self-conscious of the brevity of their his-

These views of Portage, Wisconsin, evoke the town in which Turner was born and raised—the neat Federal-style buildings succeeding the raw trappings of the frontier by only a few years. Above: canal and mills, c. 1870; below: church and residences, 1856.

Turner's parents and birthplace. His father, Andrew Jackson Turner (1832–1905), was a noted newspaper editor, Republican politician, and civic booster. His mother, Mary Hanford Turner (1838–1906), is pictured prior to her marriage. The Turner house in the Fifth Ward of Portage was famed for "a two-ton boulder that graced the front yard." The family occupied this house until 1882, when they moved to a larger brick structure on Franklin Street.

The Class of 1876, pictured in front of Bascom Hall on the University of Wisconsin campus about five years before young Fred Turner entered the university.

View of Madison, c. 1875 (capitol on horizon at left).

Frederick Jackson Turner as an incoming freshman at the University of Wisconsin, 1881. (Turner entered the university in the fall of 1878 but contracted spinal meningitis in 1879 and was forced to undergo a long convalescence at home.)

Turner's mentor and predecessor on the University of Wisconsin history faculty, William Francis Allen, pictured with Allen's son Will in the study of their home on Langdon Street in Madison, c. 1887. Professor Allen's library was larger than some public library collections of the time.

Turner, pictured about 1892 in his office in the State Historical Society quarters in the state capitol, Madison. This was roughly three years after Turner joined the faculty of the University of Wisconsin, and a year prior to his address in Chicago.

Turner's American history seminar in the State Historical Society library in the state capitol, c. 1893–1894. (Turner is seated, second from right.)

Frederick Jackson Turner, c. 1905, or about five years before he left Wisconsin for Harvard University.

WHi(X3)913

WHi(X3)904

WHi(X3)3210

Family snapshots of Frederick Jackson Turner and his wife Caroline and their children at their residence at 629 Frances Street, on Lake Mendota, Madison. The Turners built the house in 1894 and occupied it until 1910.

WHi(X3)887

WHi(X3)1184

WHi(X3)3211

WHi(X3)871

The Turners first visited Hancock Point, Maine, in 1903. They vacationed there periodically from then on, purchasing a vacation cottage ("The Moorings") in 1919. Turner loved the outdoors and was often photographed in the forest or on the stream—even on horseback, as at Wagon Wheel Gap, Utah, in 1902.

WHi(X3)1185

Turner in his Western mode, on frozen Lake Mendota and (in stern of boat) on Lake Wisconsin.

Frederick Jackson Turner as professor of American history at Harvard, December, 1917.

tory. The frontier thesis provided an American past as grand as that of England or any continental power, an American landscape as spectacular as any in the world, and heroes, heroines, and myths the equal of any in Europe. Moreover, state and local historians for the first time understood where their work fit into the broader context of American history and could take pride in the contributions of their subjects. Even the word frontier became a critical part of the nation's rhetoric: Americans thereafter spoke in terms of our frontiers in science, space, and knowledge, always on the assumption that the frontier held the promise of unique opportunities for progress and reward. And when the American economy failed during the Great Depression of the 1930's, or when the environmental crisis of the 1970's became evident, or when the oil shortages of that decade befell the nation, politicians and sages pointed to our closed frontier as an explanation for the possible decline in the quality of our lives.

Following the publication of "The Significance of the Frontier in American History," Turner wrote many essays that elaborated on his basic theme.[9] They earned for him recognition and rewards; he was the peer of any historian of his generation. He was lured away from the University of Wisconsin by Harvard, and after his retirement was recruited as the premier scholar at the Henry E. Huntington Library. Turner's later writings proved to be as innovative as the early work done at Wisconsin. He espoused a theory of sectionalism that helped explain the coming of the Civil War. By the time of his death in 1932 he was not only the most widely respected scholar of his time but also among the most admired. (He won a Pulitzer Prize posthumously in 1933 for his book *The Significance of Sections in American History*.)[10] Yet always he remained an affable citizen of Portage, Wisconsin, who never lost his personal democratic touch despite his success.

As Turner himself would have predicted when he wrote "The Significance of History," changing times and moods in academic and public life inevitably produced a rising host of criticism of his frontier thesis, especially as spelled out in his early work and as overstated by his loyal but less prudent followers. Critics contended that Turner's argument was too simple and that he overlooked or left unaccounted for powerful elements in American life.[11] They also felt that he treated American society as a monolith, ignoring the contributions of recent immigrant groups. Turner, many insisted, had merely substituted the idea of environment when what he espoused was a crude materialistic determinism. Historians with newer concerns—race, slavery, law, literature, art, diplomacy, immigration, and the city—argued that the Turner thesis did not address crucial questions. Still others believed that his history was a rationale for

American chauvinism in an age of imperialism. Turner, who had attacked tribal history, was denounced as a patron of ultra-nationalism. Many also objected to his prose style, insisting that it was so colorful that it obscured rather than clarified his meaning.

Perhaps the most damaging indictment came from scholars who challenged Turner's definition of democracy as a product of the frontier experience and denounced the negative implications of his thesis for American institutions in a post-frontier era. No critic, however, has ever asserted that the existence of a vast undeveloped hinterland had no effect on the nation's progress.

For every attack by critics there were, of course, responses, and scholars have not ended, and probably will not end, their debate over the validity of his argument to explain America's pre-World War I past. During his lifetime, Turner rarely replied to his critics, but his students and disciples kept up the good fight, defending the essential points of his remarkable essay. Turner's ideas, moreover, were picked up and applied effectively in other fields, especially what was called his "pioneer-succession model" of institutional change. When Turner noted that the earliest frontier type was capable of adapting to unique hardships and was later displaced by less hardy types when the physical environment had been tamed, his insight for example suggested to botanists an organic model where a single plant species often settles in an unoccupied, inhospitable habitat, such as a barren rock, and as the seasons come and go and humus accumulates, the rock's surface is scored by plant acids, and enough soil is formed for the ingress of another species that could not have earlier survived on the barren rock but now thrives and forces the original pioneer stock to seek a new home. Turner's language, images, and ways of thinking have in this and other instances been thoroughly assimilated by the academic community.

"The Significance of the Frontier in American History" is now a classic. It is as often read as a piece of literature as it is as a theory about American history in the nineteenth century. Turner's rhetoric—his style of composition—is now seen as part of the argument itself.[12] But the primary importance of the essay remains its statement explaining the agricultural society that determined the values of nineteenth-century America. More recent historical theories—whether based on race, modernization, Puritanism, abundance, Marxism, or consensus and conflict—have simply failed to capture the imagination of the whole scholarly community or the general public. Newer methods for the study of history, especially those that employ computers, have resulted in intriguing insights, but they have not created any overall hypotheses to explain national development. (In fact, many of the methodological innovations relying on computers are patterned after questions that Turner asked years ago but did not have the technology to answer.) The "frontier thesis" is far from a complete explanation of American history, but it remains a most appealing one for people who want to ask larger questions about American history and appreciate straightforward and common-sense answers.

Implicit in Turner's thesis, even stripped of its scholarly dimensions, are ideas that have meaning for our time. Although Turner stressed the importance of the physical environment in shaping human institutions and the eventual triumph of men and women over the natural world in which they live, his work reminds readers that people can and do change the world in which they live. There are relationships between society and the physical world that cannot be ignored, except at the peril of the race. Today Americans may still be too ready to accept the results of mining, farming, and lumbering on the nineteenth-century landscape, but they are increasingly aware that to survive on the continent communities must live in greater harmony with their surroundings.

Turner's views about the epochal nature of the closing of the frontier—the elimination of the frontier line in the 1890 census—are worth remembering today because they emphasize as nothing else can that a society must always afford economic opportunity for its members or risk the loss of its democratic institutions.[13] It is a theme that every President since Franklin D. Roosevelt has echoed. Turner may have sounded a pessimistic note, but his words also had an optimistic dimension in that he believed the choices were with the people.

Turner's theory of democracy was deeply rooted in the ideas of economic opportunity. His is the pragmatic democracy of Andrew Jackson rather than the theoretical democracy of Thomas Jefferson, even though he heralded the achievements of the self-sufficient farmer. It is based as much on what Turner saw growing up in Portage as what his research disclosed about frontier peoples establishing and managing their own governments through direct participation. Yet Turner also recognized that frontier people placed great trust in a strong national government that could serve a vital need when projects were too large for local groups to nurture. Turner in no way escaped the values of his time, but his trust in public participation in government, in the role of the national state, and in the critical importance of economic opportunity for people who have not succeeded are ideas that have a powerful ring today.

Turner's frontier settler is inextricably linked to his perception of national identity and character. His frontier was a nationalizing force, which in some way compelled diverse immigrant sectional groups to accommodate to each other and blend into something unique—neither northerner nor southerner, neither alien nor Yankee, but something distinctly American with a common and shared culture. It is somewhat ironic to see that Turner's style of frontier nationalism is again in vogue, especially when many Americans are busy seeking their "roots" and defending the values of a pluralistic society. The American public embraces a unique common culture that accepts pluralism and sees it as part of a national identity that has a frontier origin.

Almost a century has elapsed since Turner began his teaching and writing career at Wisconsin. Yet the essay he wrote for school teachers and the speech he gave at the Chicago World's Fair are far from lost or dated documents. His ideas are still worth considering, both by professional historians and the general public, because they offer Americans a usable past and a basis from which to look into the future. His essays, still fresh and lively, are now part of the American heritage that he so shrewdly analyzed.

Young Fred Turner

Ray A. Billington

◆

OUR PURPOSE is to explore a brief period in the life of one of Wisconsin's most distinguished scholars, and through this the genesis of an idea that has over the past three-quarters of a century revitalized the teaching of our nation's history, plunged usually placid historians into a generation of bitter controversy, allowed statesmen to rationalize such divergent concepts as "rugged individualism" and the "welfare state," and significantly altered the image of the American people held by themselves and the world. The scholar was Frederick Jackson Turner; the idea, his "frontier hypothesis."

This startingly new concept was revealed to the historical world in 1893 when Turner read his now-famous paper on "The Significance of the Frontier in American History" to a gathering of the clan in Chicago. His purpose was not to explain the *similarities* between Europe and America, which then occupied the attention of scholars, but the *differences.* These, he believed, were due in part to the unusual environment in which the civilization of the United States grew to maturity. The most unique feature of this environment was the existence for three centuries of an area of unoccupied land on the yonder edge of the settled portions of the continent which constantly drew men westward. There primitive conditions of life corroded past customs and subtly altered behavioral patterns: the abundance of natural resources blurred class distinctions by allowing the energetic and skillful to rise in the social scale; the absence of community restraints encouraged lawlessness and individualism; the lack of any prior leadership structure stimulated the emergence of democratic practices; the necessity for hard work glorified materialism and generated suspicion of intellectualism or esthetic pursuits; the plenitude of natural resources bred habits of wastefulness; the uniqueness of the problems demanding solution fostered inventiveness and a willingness to innovate. Many of the traits distinguishing Americans from their European cousins, Turner believed, could be traced in part to their frontiering past.

When young Fred J. Turner, as he then signed himself, formulated this stimulating interpretation of American history he was slightly more than thirty years old, with a Johns Hopkins doctorate only three years behind him, and with his teaching career at the University of Wisconsin still in its infancy. He was, in other words, in that stage of academic development where most emerging scholars would be content with laborious monographic publications, distinguished more by their multitudinous footnotes than by their freshness of interpretation. Why did Turner differ so markedly from his colleagues of that day—or this? Whence came the inspiration that allowed him to formulate a concept so startlingly original that historians of today find it as thought-provoking as did his own generation?

Studies in the psychology of creativity suggest that new ideas are the product of a multitude of influences, fused into final form by a flash of creative brilliance. This certainly was the case with Turner's frontier hypothesis. An examination of his reading notes, preserved today in the Huntington Library, indicates that he was influenced by the intellectual atmosphere in which he lived, by reports of the Census Bureau, by the writings of geographers and political economists, and especially by the studies of such European social philosophers as the Italian Achille Loria and the Englishman Walter Bagehot. Yet Turner himself believed that his frontier concept stemmed in part from the Wisconsin of his boyhood, and the evidence tends to support his view.

Frederick Jackson Turner was born at Portage, Columbia County, on November 14, 1861, the son of Andrew Jackson Turner and Mary Hanford Turner. Ample evidence exists to show the enduring influence of his parents on his life and thought. His mother, a former schoolteacher, maintained a cultured atmosphere in the Turner household and guarded her chicks with all the fussiness of a mother hen, but it was to his father that young Fred Turner looked for guidance and advice. A man of strength and firmness, Andrew Jackson Turner had drifted westward from his birthplace at Schuyler Falls, New York, reaching Portage in 1855 with only a dime in his pockets, but with limitless ambition and a desire to grow up with a new country. There he found work as a printer, and there he prospered until he was able, in the year that his son was born, to purchase the newspaper on which he had labored and merged it with a rival as the *Wisconsin State Register*. From that time on the elder Turner divided his time between publishing and Republican politics, serving for a time as a member of the state legislature, as a member of the state railroad commission, and as mayor of Portage. He also dabbled in railroad promotion as one of the founders of the Portage and Lake Superior Railroad Company, and found time to establish a considerable reputation as a genealogist and local historian.[1]

Strangely enough, the facets of his father's many-sided career that most impressed young Fred Turner were not those that had to do with genealogy or history, for he showed as little interest in his family's sturdy New England ancestry as he did in the elder Turner's antiquarian writings. "I do not," he wrote in his latter years, "know how far the family disposition may have affected my interest in frontier history—not much, I suspect, for it was only in my father's later years that I was made familiar with the genealogical lines, an amusement which he took up in his old age."[2] Instead the father's political activities not only fascinated the son but provided him with an understanding of politics that endured throughout his lifetime. From the elder Turner young Fred learned of the many ethnic groups whose votes must be solicited, of the constant need for compromise and adjustment if elections were to be won, of the importance of committees and other behind-the-scenes activities in the political process. "I have always felt," he remembered later, "that I understood party politics very much better from having seen, at close range and from the inside, his own interests in that subject and his skill in shepherding the many nationalities that lived in Columbia County."[3] These lessons were to stand the future historian in good stead when he began his analysis of the underlying forces shaping past political behavior.

If Turner's parents played only a minor role in moulding the historian of the future, the same cannot be said of the town and countryside in which he grew to maturity. Often in his later years he recalled with obvious nostalgia the scenes of his boyhood in Portage: the roughness of that pioneer town in its early infancy, the lumbering activities nearby, the encounters with Indian bands on canoe trips through the virgin forests. That indoctrination into frontier life, Turner steadfastly maintained, permanently influenced his historical concepts and planted in his mind the germ of the frontier hypothesis.

"I have," he wrote Carl Becker in 1925, "poled down the Wisconsin [River] in a dugout with Indian guides from 'Grandfather Bull Falls,' through virgin forests of balsam firs, seeing deer in the river,—antlered beauties who watched us come down with curious eyes and then broke for the tall timber,—hearing the squaws in their village on the high bank talk their low treble to the bass of our Indian polesman,—feeling that I belonged to it all. I have seen a lynched man hanging from a tree when I came home from school in Portage, have played around old Fort Winne-

bago at its outskirts, have seen the red-shirted Irish raftsmen *take* the
town when they tied up and came ashore, have plodded up the 'pinery'
road that ran past our house to the pine woods of Northern Wisconsin,
have seen Indians come in on their ponies to buy paint and ornaments
and sell their furs; have stumbled on their camp on the Baraboo [River],
where dried pumpkins were hung up, and cooking muskrats were in the
kettle, and an Indian family were bathing in the river—the frontier in
that sense, you see, was real to me, and when I studied history I did not
keep my personal experiences in a water-tight compartment away from
my studies."[4] Surely one reared amidst such scenes must realize that
there was a difference between Americans who had been bred on frontiers and Europeans with no such experience.

This was especially the case because Turner's memory was as fallible
as that of most humans, endowing the recalled scenes of his boyhood
with a romance that they scarcely possessed. His description of the frontier-like glamor of the Baraboo written in 1925 to Becker bears little
relation to another account of that same adventure penned in 1888 when
events were still fresh in his mind: "Jim Cole and I used to go fishing
there. One day we left our lunch pail on the bridge and started upstream
to catch catfish, dodging rattlesnakes and eating chokeberries on the
way. When we returned, hungry, footsore, fishless toward evening—the
dinner pail was gone! Off in the woods there was an Indian village where
the men were cleaning their guns, and the boys making bows and ar-
rows, while the squaws were boiling some muskrats. We did not accept
their invitation to dine, but started on our four-mile trip back. Half way
there we were overtaken and passed by the Indian villagers with their
camp and all the men on horseback,—the little ponies fairly hidden
under the traps and big Indians, while the squaws, each burdened with a
patient-faced papoose tied to a board and strapped to their backs,
trudged on foot. One bloodthirsty redskin saluted us from a distance
with the assurance 'Heap good pail of grub'! We never went fishing in
the Baraboo again."[5] Distance lends enchantment, in time as well as
space.

Yet nostalgic memories did haunt Turner, and he returned to them
after listening to an illustrated lecture on Mississippi River towns: "It
carried me back to my boyhood days, when the Wisconsin River rafts
came down and tied up at Portage, when the red-shirted, profane, hard-
drinking, and virile Irishmen came ashore and took possession. Talk
about he-men and red blood! They had it, 100%—. Then there was the
inviting 'pinery road' that ran past our house to the pine forests of the
upper Wisconsin. I wonder now why I didn't start off some day and 'see
the world,' either on a raft, or hiking up the road! But I wasn't a trail

maker, in spite of my later tastes. . . . I remember when with my father I took one of the first trains through the woods of northern Wisconsin to Lake Superior,—a narrow aisle cut like a gash through the wonderful white pine forest. And I remember a voyage down the Wisconsin, poled by Indians in a dugout from near Wausau, and hearing a duet-like conversation between the boatmen and the squaws as we passed their Indian village—the guttural of the buck and the sweet, clear laughing treble of the squaw. I remember the antlered deer who stood at the bend among the balsam firs, drinking at the river's edge, and how close we got to him in our silent canoe before he snorted and broke for cover."[6]

That unspoiled countryside of Columbia and Marquette counties, with its frontier hamlets and its Indian villages where past and present were curiously joined, certainly placed its stamp on Turner's historical thinking. So, too, did the medley of racial groups that he remembered as peopling Portage and nearby communities. "There was an Irish ward," he recalled later, "into which we boys ventured only in companies. There was a Pomeranian ward where the women wore wooden shoes, kerchiefs on their heads, red woolen petticoats &c and drove their community's cows to a common pasture in the marsh lands which these people bought. Their dikes and drains made homesites in a neighboring marsh, which was almost a lake in my boyhood. There were Norwegian settlements, Scotch towns, Welsh, and Swiss communities in the county. . . . In the city itself we had all types from a Negro family named Turner, to an Irish 'keener' who looked like a Druid and whose shrill voice could be heard over impossible spaces when an Irish soul departed. . . . It was a town with a real collection of types from all the world, Yankees from Maine & Vermont, New York Yankees, Dutchmen from the Mohawk, braw curlers from the Highlands, Southerners—all kinds. They mixed, too. And respected and fought each other."[7] Here was a human environment different from any that Europe knew; surely this ethnological conglomeration would place its stamp on the people just as did the physical environment.

So Turner believed as he recalled his childhood days. Yet the question remains: did his memory play tricks upon him, endowing the scenes of his youth with frontier-like traits simply because of his own later interest in the pioneer era? Was Portage really a half-civilized village of Irish brawlers, lynchings, and Indian traders? Or was it an orderly community that had graduated from its frontier past into mature respectability? Actually the truth lay somewhere between, but the early history of Columbia County suggests that Turner was surprisingly correct in his recollections and that the quasi-frontier atmosphere in which he was reared did influence his later thinking.

Trappers and traders had long camped along the portageway between the Fox and Wisconsin rivers, and nearby Fort Winnebago had
been the center of a cluster of cabins since its founding, but the village of
Portage was scarcely a decade old when Turner was born there in 1861.
A traveler who passed by in 1849 reported only one house and a store
on the bluffs above the river, and a ramshackle cabin or two belonging to
traders on the flats below.[8] Indians were still common in the neighbor-
hood; the Menominee did not cede their last Columbia County lands
until 1849, and the Winnebago, while surrendering their claims in 1837,
clung to their camps along the Baraboo River until 1873, when the last
bands were removed by federal troops. Young Turner probably saw the
dejected tribesmen as they were marched through the Portage streets
and loaded on railroad cars for the long journey to their Nebraska reser-
vation. Government surveys of the ceded native lands proceeded rapidly
enough, but not until 1845 were the Winnebago hunting grounds
opened to settlers while portions of the Menominee lands were not
ready for sale until 1851.[9]

By this time Portage and its nearby countryside were ready to enter
upon the boom period of spectacular growth that characterized many
frontier towns. Speculation was encouraged by two developments that
promised fabulous profits to shrewd investors. One was the promised
completion of a canal between the Fox and Wisconsin rivers, a prospect
that conjured up visions of Great Lakes-to-Mississippi steamboat traffic
with untold business for merchants whose establishments lay along the
route. Work was progressing rapidly as the decade of the 1850's
dawned, under the stimulus of a land grant received from the federal
government in 1849, and even the failure of the canal to operate success-
fully when it was opened in 1851 did not dim speculative hopes.[10]
Equally stimulating to the get-rich-quick promoters so common in frontier communities was the prospect of early railroad connections with
eastern markets. A congressional land grant of 1856 quickened their expectations, and their dreams were realized in 1857 when the La Crosse
and Milwaukee Railroad reached Portage, only to succumb to the panic
of that year before being completed to La Crosse. A decade later a second land grant endowed the Portage and Superior Railroad Company to
build between Portage and Lake Superior, a project that was not completed until 1877. Portage was in the meantime connected with Madison
by the Madison and Portage Railroad Company.[11] Each of these projects
stirred the speculative spirit among those who dreamed of making Portage the transportation hub of central Wisconsin, and each stimulated a
rush of settlers to the burgeoning little village.

The results could be read in the mushrooming population statistics.

Columbia County boasted only 1,969 settlers in 1846; by 1850 it had grown to 9,565, by 1855 to 17,965, and by 1860 to 24,500.[12] Portage grew just as remarkably, especially after its incorporation as a city in 1854. Each year during the decade a new army of settlers arrived, first from Ohio, but increasingly from New York, Pennsylvania, and the New England states. As the first raw frontier stage was passed this tide was swelled by migrants from Europe, with Germany, Great Britain, and the Scandinavian countries contributing the largest numbers. To many of these newcomers the lowlands along the river's edge—inelegantly known as "The Flats"—proved unattractive. Instead they built their cabins along the brow of the semicircular hill that rose sharply from the water. For a time rivalry between "Lower Town" and "Upper Town" was intense, but when the "Upper Town" dwellers won the post office for their community the future course of Portage was made clear. Gradually during the course of the decade the mercantile establishments that had occupied the first settlers were supplemented by manufacturing concerns as the growing city showed every sign of permanent expansion.[13] "Seven years ago," wrote a traveler in 1858, "I entered Portage on a lumber-wagon, after a tedious four-day journey from Milwaukee. What is now a large, well-built city, with an enterprising population, was then an unclaimed waste, dotted by a few straggling houses. Its growth has been almost magical."[14]

This was the bustling little city where Frederick Jackson Turner was born in 1861. Portage boasted 2,879 inhabitants then, nine of them colored, the remainder about equally divided between native-born and foreign-born. Its dozens of stores and mercantile establishments, some of them housed in a handsome brick block three stories high, rivaled Milwaukee in the quality and price of their goods, belying the name of "Gougeville" that had been fastened on the town only a few years before. Its small factories hummed with activity: a four-story flour mill near the canal, an iron furnace, a steam sawmill, two breweries, a large grain elevator near the depot, and planing and chair-making establishments to utilize the plentiful lumber supplies. Travelers all noted the unusually attactive appearance of Portage, commenting especially on the cream-colored brick, fashioned from a local white clay, that was used in many buildings. Four years after Turner was born the city proudly opened its new courthouse, which was described as a "model of architectural neatness and simplicity," three stories high and surmounted by a colossal statue of justice with sword and scales in hand.[15]

This was the Portage in which young Fred Turner spent his youth, attending the local schools and graduating from the high school in 1878. "You were, one of his classmates later recalled, "the despair of our entire class, because, no matter how diligently we worked, we could never equal the examination marks that you had."[16] Turner was honored on graduation day by being selected to give one of the student orations. His ringing words on "The Power of the Press" must have gladdened his father's heart. "Aside from its great value as a disseminator of news," the young orator proclaimed, "the daily press is one of the greatest of civilizers and public teachers, and is a necessary adjunct of every free government. When there is perfect freedom of the Press, the people will make known their power through it, and will resist all tendency toward oppression."[17] Uncertain health kept Turner at home for the next two years until he entered the University of Wisconsin in 1880. During that interim he apparently worked at his father's printing trade and as a reporter; he also succumbed to the lure of uniforms so universal in those post-Civil War days and joined a military company named the "Guppey Guard" after its founder. Its members, splendid in gray cloth with dark facing and gold trim, won a number of drill competitions in such distant cities as Madison.[18]

Portage continued to grow during those years that Turner knew it so well, but at a less spectacular rate than before; by 1870 its population had increased to 3,945 and by 1880 to 4,346, of whom 3,041 were native Americans and 1,305 foreign-born.[19] These changing proportions, together with the slowing rate of growth, indicated that the city's frontier era was drawing to a close. Yet there were almost daily reminders that central Wisconsin had not completely surrendered to the forces of civilization. Two men were lynched there during Turner's boyhood. One, William H. Spain, was forcibly taken from the law officers by a mob in the fall of 1869 after he had shot a man to death on the street, and was hanged to a nearby tree. Another, Patrick Wildrick, a notorious outlaw and highwayman, was spirited from the local jail a few nights later by a group that acted with all the precision of a vigilance committee. His body was found hanging from another tree when Portage awakened the next morning.[20] Nor did Turner's memory play him false when he later remembered the wild Irish raftsmen who regularly "took over" the town. As late as 1877 between 140 and 200 million board feet of lumber passed Portage on its way to the Mississippi River. The great rafts, formed at one of the 107 sawmills that dotted the upper Wisconsin River, had been floated over an almost constant succession of rapids before they reached Portage, with the raftsmen breaking them into small "rapid pieces" for each descent and laboriously regrouping them in the short stretches of calmer water. Little wonder that they were ready for a spree at Portage before the last, less-arduous phase of their journey.[21] These were sights to quicken the pulse of any normal boy, and Turner never forgot them.

He was brought even closer to frontier days in his constant wanderings about the countryside in quest of new trout streams or calm lakes where bass and pickerel would rise to his fly. "I have," he wrote his fiancée on one such expedition, "been flitting from lake to lake, and stream to stream; here trailing a fly upon the placid water and hearing the whir of the reel as a bass leaped out and shook himself—and here strolling along a winding brook through meadows, whipping the eddies at the bends until a flash and a quiver tell me of a trout struck. Of all the beautiful things a gleaming, gold and crimson trout throwing himself out of water after a fly is the most beautiful—almost."[22] This was the lure that sent the young Turner roaming far: to Caledonia and Cambria and Lewiston in Columbia County where fish-filled lakes abounded; into Marquette County where the tiny village of Montello was one of his favorite haunts; northward along the Baraboo and the Wisconsin River as far as Big Bull Falls.

On these extended expeditions he had an opportunity to view at close hand a social order in a state of flux. Columbia County was growing steadily; its population increased from 24,500 in 1860 to 28,000 in 1880. Nearby Marquette County where he spent so much time was still closer to nature; its population totaled only 8,300 in 1860 and 8,900 in 1880. Here were the isolated farm and new settlements typical of all frontiers; here, too, Turner could observe the changes that occurred as newcomers arrived from the East or from Europe to nudge prior inhabitants on to still newer frontiers. Of the 20,500 native-born inhabitants of Columbia County in 1880, 2,674 had come from New York, 300 from Pennsylvania, nearly 800 from New England, and 390 from other states of the Old Northwest. Germany had contributed almost half of the 7,500 foreign-born, with England and Wales adding 1,500, Ireland more than 1,000, and the Scandinavian countries about 900. Marquette County offered a similar study of racial mixtures, with the 1,700 Germans among its 2,800 foreign-born forming the largest incoming group.[23]

All of this dynamic change made a lasting impression on Turner. He noted the formation of racial communities: the large number of Scots at Caledonia, the predominance of Welsh at Cambria where a traditional *eisteddfod* festival was held yearly, and the many Germans in the farm country about Montello.[24] "For the past few days," he wrote from that Marquette County town in 1886, "we have been camped on a trout brook some twenty miles north of here. We had a gloriously good time! Our tent was pitched just where we could be sent to sleep by the low rumble of a little mill wheel; surrounded by great elms; the water ice-cold; milk, eggs and butter in abundance at the German farm house nearby. He couldn't speak a word of English so I had a little taste of continental life, and had to brush up on my Teutonic. I had the pleasure of getting the biggest string of trout which was a luxury I hadn't before enjoyed."[25] Two years later he recorded a similar experience: "Everybody is German here. It was only owing to my limited smattering of German that we were able to buy eggs and grasshoppers this morning from Ernst and Emil, the two promising young Germans who live here."[26] No one of Turner's sensitivity to social change could live long in such a fluid social order without pondering the effect of these ethnic comings and goings on the structure of society.

The fruits of his observations, and of his boyhood in a country newly emerged from its frontier past, would seem to be twofold. On the one hand, Turner's interest in the West as a subject for historical study was permanently awakened; on the other, he experienced at least a glimmer of the truth concerning the frontier's impact on American society as he watched the displacement of one ethnic group by another in the farm areas near his trout streams.

That Turner's interest in western history was excited by the scenes of his boyhood seems beyond dispute. Certainly he testified to that fact many times in later life. "Possibly," he wrote in 1928, "my interest in the frontier was caused by the fact that I was born in Portage, Wisconsin, at a time when the region was in the later stages of a frontier community."[27] A short time later he returned to this theme in another letter to a friend: "In a general way, I may say that my interest in the West was due to the fact that I was born in Wisconsin in the period when it was still passing through quasi-frontier conditions; and that, in part, this interest was the result of a feeling, while a student at Johns Hopkins, that the dynamic influence in American history derived from the expansion of our population into the interior from the Atlantic Coast had been insufficiently recognized and was still practically neglected in the understanding of the United States. My essay on the 'Frontier' was a protest against the tendencies of the eastern historians at the time it was written."[28]

These latter-day statements in no way exaggerated the influence of Wisconsin's environment on young Turner's questioning mind. The embryo scholar who had watched men adjust to the unfamiliar environment of a new land, and who had observed the succession of racial types that intruded on the wilderness, was hardly one to accept the commonly held dictum of his day that American society had been transplanted unchanged from its Germanic place of origin. "I am," he wrote in 1887 while a student at the University of Wisconsin, "placed in a *new* society which is just beginning to realize that it has made a place for itself by mastering the wilderness and peopling the prairie, and is now ready to take its great course in universal history. It is something of a compensation to be among the advance guard of new social ideas and among a people whose destiny is all unknown. The west looks to the future, the east toward the past."[29]

The challenge of such concepts determined Turner to dedicate his scholarly career to the study of the West even before his Johns Hopkins experience drove him to rebel against traditional historical concepts. "I hope," he wrote his father in 1885, "I can get time to work out the early Green Bay fur trade history. It would be a chapter of interest in Wisconsin history."[30] Turner's first published work, a paper prepared when he was in his junior year at the university, was a "History of the 'Grignon Tract' on the Portage of the Fox and Wisconsin Rivers"; his master's thesis and doctoral dissertation dealt with the fur trade in Wisconsin.[31] These were only a few of the dozens of projects that quickened his interest. The Commonplace Book that, in the fashion of the day, he kept as a student at Wisconsin was filled with jotted notations on subjects that he longed to investigate. "Collate facts showing the settlement of Wis[consin]," he wrote in 1886. "Date of each perm[anent] settlement in State—Causes—Conclusions."[32] Or again: "Investigate land holding peasantry about Madison (e.g.) just as one would from the remains of ancient land systems (Census—Ag[ricultural] Reports—Talks) etc. How many acres average? What kind houses live in? Food? Manners—sports etc."[33] Or still again: "Need of Study of Foreign groups. . . Votes by districts. Why are Nor[wegians] rep[ublicans], Irish dem[ocrats]."[34] Turner would never have asked himself such questions if he had been reared in thickly settled Massachusetts or Virginia. The evolving social order fascinated him, and helped stimulate those conjectures from which the frontier hypothesis was to emerge.

Turner was not alone interested in the West by his boyhood environment; that environment helped reveal to him the nature of the frontier process and its importance in American Life. He found his clue in the changing nature of society as German immigrants flooded over his fishing haunts in Marquette and Columbia counties. "I find," he wrote his revered teacher, Professor William Francis Allen, from Portage in 1888, "that this country is becoming Germanized. . . . They are dispossessing whole townships of Americans and introducing the customs and farming methods of the fatherland."[35] Here was a fertile field for conjecture. What happened to the displaced Yankees? Were Germanic customs reproduced unchanged on Wisconsin's oak openings? Or did the environment alter them in some subtle but hitherto unobserved manner?

Turner returned to these questions a year later when he was a graduate student at Johns Hopkins University, immersing himself in social and economic theory under the guidance of Herbert Baxter Adams, Richard

T. Ely, and Woodrow Wilson. "Wisconsin," he wrote Professor Allen, "is like a palimpsest. The mound builders wrote their record and passed away. The State was occupied . . . by the most various peoples of Indian race. Then came the French. Then a wave of Northern New York and Vermont fur traders—those who lived near the Lake Champlain route or the Great Lakes caught that fur-trading spirit. At nearly this time came the miners from the South. Then the immigration from the *New York parallel* again on the farm lands. Now begins the state's policy of attracting immigration. And see the effect on the legislative policy of Wisconsin (1) in its land grants to railroads, and (2) in the quick and ruinously cheap sale of its educational lands." The railroads, he felt, especially needed study, for they changed the character of the population by inducing westward migration.[36]

These successive waves of immigrants, Turner reasoned, would alter the social order, for he had learned in Professor Ely's courses that intruding lower types of settlers normally drove out existing higher types because their lower living standard allowed them to profit by selling more of the goods they produced. The inevitable result, he felt, would be the "Germanizing" of large portions of the state. Yet there was no cause for alarm, as pioneer conditions would alter the German intruders as they had those who came before. "I think," he wrote, "peasant proprietorship is not being weakened by these German settlers. The quick settlement of lands in small farms has, I judge, prevented the absorbtion of much territory into great estates. The population is on the whole a physically sturdy one. . . . I think that the German dispossession of the Irish in Marquette has at any rate increased the economic value of the country, and has substituted Lutherans for Catholics."[37]

Young Fred Turner was still a long way from his frontier hypothesis when he wrote those words early in 1889, but he was unquestionably following the pathway that would lead him to that theory. He was aware of the fluidity of the social order in a new country, changing constantly with the arrival of successive migratory waves. He had recognized that the presence of available cheap land would prevent the accumulation of vast estates such as those of Europe, and thus check the emergence of a peasant class. And, most important of all, he had learned that the society of his native state was an evolving organism, changing before his very eyes. This practical demonstration of the theories that he had learned from his teachers was certain to affect his thinking, and to focus his attention on the emerging West where the evolution was most rapid.

The time had come when Turner was to look beyond his native state for inspiration, and to build his concepts on the broader theoretical basis that came with his mastery of history, political economy, and geography. But his early years in Wisconsin had made an indelible impression upon him. He had learned to love the West with its turbulence and its bold spirit of innovation; he had realized that social evolution was a living experience instead of an abstract theory embalmed in textbooks; he had accepted the uniqueness of backwoods society and the importance of its environment in shaping the lives of transplanted newcomers. Wisconsin was ready to share Frederick Jackson Turner with a wider world of scholarship, but only after it had prepared him to endow that world with a stimulating new historical theory.

The Significance of the Frontier in American History[1]

Frederick Jackson Turner

◆

IN A RECENT BULLETIN of the superintendent of the census for 1890 appear these significant words: "Up to and including 1880 the country had a frontier of settlement, but at present the unsettled area has been so broken into by isolated bodies of settlement that there can hardly be said to be a frontier line. In the discussion of its extent, its westward movements, etc., it cannot, therefore, any longer have a place in the census reports."[2] This brief official statement marks the closing of a great historic movement. Up to our own day American history has been in a large degree the history of the colonization of the Great West. The existence of an area of free land, its continuous recession, and the advance of American settlement westward, explain American development. Behind institutions, behind constitutional forms and modifications, lie the vital forces that call these organs into life, and shape them to meet changing conditions. Now, the peculiarity of American institutions is, the fact that they have been compelled to adapt themselves to the changes of an expanding people—to the changes involved in crossing a continent, in winning a wilderness, and in developing at each area of this progress out of the primitive economic and political conditions of the frontier into the complexity of city life. Said Calhoun in 1817, "We are great, and rapidly—I was about to say fearfully—growing!"[3] So saying, he touched the distinguishing feature of American life. All peoples show development: the germ theory of politics has been sufficiently emphasized. In the case of most nations, however, the development has occurred in a limited area; and if the nation has expanded, it has met other growing peoples whom it has conquered. But in the case of the United States we have a different phenomenon. Limiting our attention to the Atlantic coast, we have the familiar phenomenon of the evolution of institutions in a limited area, such as the rise of representative government; the differentia-

26

tion of simple colonial governments into complex organs; the progress from primitive industrial society, without division of labor, up to manufacturing civilization. But we have in addition to this a *recurrence of the process of evolution in each western area reached in the process of expansion.* Thus American development has exhibited not merely advance along a single line, but a return to primitive conditions on a continually advancing frontier line, and a new development for that area. American social development has been continually beginning over again on the frontier. This perennial rebirth, this fluidity of American life, this expansion westward with its new opportunities, its continuous touch with the simplicity of primitive society, furnish the forces dominating American character. The true point of view in the history of this nation is not the Atlantic coast, it is the Great West. Even the slavery struggle, which is made so exclusive an object of attention by writers like Professor von Holst, occupies its important place in American history because of its relation to westward expansion.

In this advance, the frontier is the outer edge of the wave—the meeting point between savagery and civilization. Much has been written about the frontier from the point of view of border warfare and the chase, but as a field for the serious study of the economist and the historian it has been neglected.

What is the frontier? It is not the European frontier—a fortified boundary line running through dense populations. The most significant thing about it is, that it lies at the hither edge of free land. In the census reports it is treated as the margin of that settlement which has a density of two or more to the square mile. The term is an elastic one, and for our purpose does not need sharp definition. We shall consider the whole frontier belt, including the Indian country and the outer margin of the "settled area" of the census reports. This paper will make no attempt to treat the subject exhaustively; its aim is simply to call attention to the frontier as a fertile field for investigation, and to suggest some of the problems which arise in connection with it.

In the settlement of America we have to observe how European life entered the continent, and how America modified and developed that life, and reacted on Europe. Our early history is the study of European germs developing in an American environment. Too exclusive attention has been paid by institutional students to the Germanic origins, too little to the American factors. Now, the frontier is the line of most rapid and effective Americanization. The wilderness masters the colonist. It finds him a European in dress, industries, tools, modes of travel, and thought. It takes him from the railroad car and puts him in the birch canoe. It strips off the garments of civilization, and arrays him in the hunting shirt and the moccasin. It puts him in the log cabin of the Cherokee and the Iroquois, and runs an Indian palisade around him. Before long he has gone to planting Indian corn and plowing with a sharp stick; he shouts the war cry and takes the scalp in orthodox Indian fashion. In short, at the frontier the environment is at first too strong for the man. He must accept the conditions which it furnishes, or perish, and so he fits himself into the Indian clearings and follows the Indian trails. Little by little he transforms the wilderness, but the outcome is not the old Europe, not simply the development of Germanic germs, any more than the first phenomenon was a case of reversion to the Germanic mark. The fact is, that here is a new product that is American. At first, the frontier was the Atlantic coast. It was the frontier of Europe in a very real sense. Moving westward, the frontier became more and more American. *As successive terminal moraines result from successive glaciations, so each frontier leaves its traces behind it, and when it becomes a settled area the region still partakes of the frontier characteristics.* Thus the advance of the frontier has meant a steady movement away from the influence of Europe, a steady growth of independence on American lines. And to study this advance, the men who grew up under these conditions, and the political, economic and social results of it, is to study the really American part of our history.

STAGES OF FRONTIER ADVANCE.

In the course of the seventeenth century the frontier was advanced up the Atlantic river courses, just beyond the "fall line," and the tidewater region became the settled area. In the first half of the eighteenth century another advance occurred. Traders followed the Delaware and Shawnese Indians to the Ohio as early as the end of the first quarter of the century.[4] Gov. Spottswood, of Virginia, made an expedition in 1714 across the Blue Ridge. The end of the first quarter of the century saw the advance of the Scotch-Irish and the Palatine Germans up the Shenandoah Valley into the western part of Virginia, and along the Piedmont region of the Carolinas.[5] The Germans in New York pushed the frontier of settlement up the Mohawk to German Flats.[6] In Pennsylvania the town of Bedford indicates the line of settlement. Settlements had begun on New River, a branch of the Kanawha, and on the sources of the Yadkin and French Broad.[7] The king attempted to arrest the advance by his proclamation of 1763,[8] forbidding settlements beyond the sources of the rivers flowing into the Atlantic; but in vain. In the period of the Revolution the frontier crossed the Alleghanies into Kentucky and Tennessee, and the upper waters of the Ohio were settled.[9] When the first census was taken in 1790, the continuous settled area was bounded by a line which ran near the coast of Maine, and included New England except a portion of Vermont and New Hampshire, New York along the Hudson and up the Mohawk about Schenectady, eastern and southern Pennsylvania, Virginia well across the Shenandoah Valley, and the Carolinas and eastern Georgia.[10] Beyond this region of continuous settlement were the small settled areas of Kentucky and Tennessee and the Ohio, with the mountains intervening between them and the Atlantic area, thus giving a new and important character to the frontier. The isolation of the region increased its peculiarly American tendencies, and the need of transportation facilities to connect it with the East called out important schemes of internal improvement, which will be noted farther on. The "West," as a self-conscious section, began to evolve.

From decade to decade distinct advances of the frontier occurred. By the census of 1820[11] the settled area included Ohio, southern Indiana and Illinois, southeastern Missouri, and about one-half of Louisiana. This settled area had surrounded Indian areas, and the management of these tribes became an object of political concern. The frontier region of the time lay along the Great Lakes, where Astor's American Fur Company operated in the Indian trade,[12] and beyond the Mississippi, where Indian traders extended their activity even to the Rocky Mountains; Florida also furnished frontier conditions. The Mississippi River region was the scene of typical frontier settlements.[13]

The rising steam navigation[14] on western waters, the opening of the Erie canal, and the westward extension of cotton culture[15] added five frontier states to the Union in this period. Grund, writing in 1836, declares: "It appears then that the universal disposition of Americans to emigrate to the western wilderness, in order to enlarge their dominion over inanimate nature, is the actual result of an expansive power which is inherent in them, and which by continually agitating all classes of society is constantly throwing a large portion of the whole population on the extreme confines of the state, in order to gain space for its development. Hardly is a new state or territory formed before the same principle manifests itself again and gives rise to a further emigration; and so it is destined to go on until a physical barrier must finally obstruct its progress."[16]

In the middle of this century the line indicated by the present eastern boundary of Indian Territory, Nebraska, and Kansas, marked the frontier of the Indian country.[17] Minnesota and Wisconsin still exhibited frontier conditions,[18] but the distinctive frontier of the period is found in California, where the gold discoveries had sent a sudden tide of adventurous miners, and in Oregon, and the settlements in Utah.[19] As the frontier had leaped over the Alleghanies, so now it skipped the Great Plains and the Rocky Mountains; and in the same way that the advance of the frontiersmen beyond the Alleghanies had caused the rise of important questions of transportation and internal improvement, so now the settlers beyond the Rocky Mountains needed means of communication with the East, and in the furnishing of these, arose the settlement of the Great Plains, and the development of still another kind of frontier life. Railroads, fostered by land grants, sent an increasing tide of immigrants into the far West. The United States army fought a series of Indian wars in Minnesota, Dakota, and the Indian Territory.

By 1880, the settled area had been pushed into northern Michigan, Wisconsin, and Minnesota, along Dakota rivers, and in the Black Hills region, and was ascending the rivers of Kansas and Nebraska. The development of mines in Colorado had drawn isolated frontier settlements into that region, and Montana and Idaho were receiving settlers. The frontier was found in these mining camps and the ranches of the great plains. The superintendent of the census for 1890 reports, as previously stated, that the settlements of the West lie so scattered over the region that there can no longer be said to be a frontier line.

In these successive frontiers we find natural boundary lines which have served to mark and to affect the characteristics of the frontiers, namely: The "fall line"; the Alleghany Mountains; the Mississippi; the Missouri where its direction approximates north and south; the line of the arid lands, approximately the 99th meridian; and the Rocky Mountains. The fall line marked the frontier of the seventeenth century; the Alleghanies that of the eighteenth; the Mississippi that of the first quarter of the nineteenth; the Missouri that of the middle of this century (omitting the California movement); and the belt of the Rocky Mountains and the arid tract, the present frontier. Each was won by a series of Indian wars.

THE FRONTIER FURNISHES A FIELD FOR COMPARATIVE STUDY OF SOCIAL DEVELOPMENT.

At the Atlantic frontier one can study the germs of processes repeated at each successive frontier. We have the complex European life, sharply precipitated by the wilderness into the simplicity of primitive conditions. The first frontier had to meet its Indian question, its question of the disposition of the public domain, of the means of intercourse with the older settlements, of the extension of political organization, of religious and educational activity. And the settlement of these and similar questions for one frontier served as a guide for the next. The American student needs not to go to the "prim little townships of Sleswick" for illustrations of the law of continuity and development. For example, he may study the origin of our land policies in the colonial land policy; he may see how the system grew by adapting the statutes to the customs of the successive frontiers.[20] He may see how the mining experience in the lead region of Wisconsin, Illinois, and Iowa was applied to the mining laws of the Rockies,[21] and how our Indian policy has been a series of experimentations on successive frontiers. Each tier of new states has found, in the older ones, material for its constitutions.[22] Each frontier has made similar contributions to American character, as will be discussed farther on.

But with all these similarities there are essential differences due to the place element and the time element. It is evident that the farming frontier of the Mississippi Valley presents different conditions from the mining frontier of the Rocky Mountains. The frontier reached by the Pacific railroad, surveyed into rectangles, guarded by the United States army, and recruited by the daily immigrant ship, moves forward at a swifter pace and in a different way than the frontier reached by the birch canoe or the pack horse. The geologist traces patiently the shores of ancient seas, maps their areas, and compares the older and the newer. It would be a work worth the historian's labors to mark these various frontiers and in detail compare one with another. Not only would there result a more adequate conception of American development and characteristics, but invaluable additions would be made to the history of society.

Loria,[23] the Italian economist, has urged the study of colonial life as an aid in understanding the stages of European development, affirming that colonial settlement is for economic science what the mountain is for geology, bringing to light primitive stratifications. "America," he says, "has the key to the historical enigma which Europe has sought for centuries in vain, and the land which has no history reveals luminously the course of universal history." He is right. The United States lies like a huge page in the history of society. Line by line as we read from west to east we find the record of social evolution. It begins with the Indian and the hunter; it goes on to tell of the disintegration of savagery by the entrance of the trader, the path-finder of civilization; we read the annals of the pastoral stage in ranch life; the exploitation of the soil by the rising of unrotated crops of corn and wheat in sparsely settled farming communities; the intensive culture of the denser farm settlement; and finally the manufacturing organization with city and factory system.[24] This page is familiar to the student of census statistics, but how little of it has been used by our historians. Each of these areas has had an influence in our economic and political history; the evolution of each into a higher stage has worked political transformations. But what constitutional historian has made any adequate attempt to interpret political facts by the light of these social areas and changes?

The Atlantic frontier was compounded of fisherman, fur trader, miner, cattle raiser and farmer. Excepting the fisherman, each type of industry was on the march toward the West, impelled by an irresistible attraction. Each passed in successive waves across the continent. Stand at Cumberland Gap and watch the procession of civilization, marching single file— the buffalo, following the trail to the salt springs, the Indian, the fur trader and hunter, the cattle raiser, the pioneer farmer,—and the frontier has passed by. Stand at South Pass in the Rockies a century later, and see the same procession with wider intervals between. The unequal rate of advance compels us to distinguish the frontier into the trader's frontier, the rancher's frontier, or the miner's frontier, and the farmer's frontier. When the mines and the cowpens were still near the fall line the traders' pack trains were tinkling across the Alleghanies, and the French on the Great Lakes were fortifying their posts, alarmed by the British trader's birch canoe. When the trappers scaled the Rockies, the farmer was still near the mouth of the Missouri.

THE INDIAN TRADER'S FRONTIER.

Why was it that the Indian trader passed so rapidly across the continent? What effects followed from the trader's frontier? The trade was coeval with American discovery. The Norsemen, Vespuccius, Verrazano, Hudson, John Smith, all trafficked for furs. The Plymouth pilgrims settled in Indian cornfields, and their first return cargo was of beaver and lumber. The records of the various New England colonies show how steadily exploration was carried into the wilderness by this trade. What is true for New England is, as would be expected, even plainer for the rest of the colonies. All along the coast from Maine to Georgia the Indian trade opened up the river courses. Steadily the trader passed westward, utilizing the older lines of French trade. The Ohio, the Great Lakes, the Mississippi, the Missouri and the Platte, the lines of western advance, were ascended by traders. They found the passes in the Rocky Mountains and guided Lewis and Clark,[25] Frémont, and Bidwell. The explanation of the rapidity of this advance is bound up with the effects of the trader on the Indian. The trading post left the unarmed tribes at the mercy of those that had purchased fire-arms—a truth which the Iroquois Indians wrote in blood, and so the remote and unvisited tribes gave eager welcome to the trader. "The savages," wrote La Salle, "take better care of us French than of their own children; from us only can they get guns and goods." This accounts for the trader's power and the rapidity of his advance. Thus the disintegrating forces of civilization entered the wilderness. Every river valley and Indian trail became a fissure in Indian society, and so that society became honeycombed. Long before the pioneer farmer appeared on the scene, primitive Indian life had passed away. The farmers met Indians armed with guns. The trading frontier, while steadily undermining Indian power by making the tribes ultimately dependent on the whites, yet, through its sale of guns, gave to the Indians increased power of resistance to the farming frontier. French colonization was dominated by its trading frontier; English colonization by its farming frontier. There was an antagonism between the two frontiers as between the two nations. Said Duquesne to the Iroquois, "Are you ignorant of the difference between the king of England and the king of France? Go see the forts that our king has established and you will see that you can still hunt under their very walls. They have been placed for your advantage in places which you frequent. The English, on the contrary, are no sooner in possession of a place than the game is driven away. The forest falls before them as they advance, and the soil is laid bare so that you can scarce find the wherewithal to erect a shelter for the night."

And yet, in spite of this opposition of the interests of the trader and the farmer, the Indian trade pioneered the way for civilization. The buffalo trail became the Indian trail, and this became the trader's "trace"; the trails widened into roads, and the roads into turnpikes, and these in turn were transformed into railroads. The same origin can be shown for the railroads of the South, the far West, and the Dominion of Canada. The trading posts reached by these trails were on the sites of Indian villages which had been placed in positions suggested by nature; and these trading posts, situated so as to command the water systems of the country, have grown into such cities as Albany, Pittsburgh, Detroit, Chicago, St. Louis, Council Bluffs, and Kansas City. Thus civilization in America has followed the arteries made by geology, pouring an even richer tide through them, until at last the slender paths of aboriginal intercourse have been broadened and interwoven into the complex mazes of modern commercial lines; the wilderness has been interpenetrated by lines of civilization, growing ever more numerous. It is like the steady growth of a complex nervous system for the originally simple, inert continent. If one would understand why we are to-day one nation, rather than a collection of isolated states, he must study this economic and social consolidation of the country. In this progress from savage conditions lie topics for the evolutionist.[26]

The effect of the Indian frontier as a consolidating agent in our history is important. From the close of the seventeenth century various intercolonial congresses have been called to treat with Indians and establish common measures of defense. Particularism was strongest in colonies with no Indian frontier. This frontier stretched along the western border like a cord of union. The Indian was a common danger, demanding united action. Most celebrated of these conferences was the Albany congress of 1754, called to treat with the Six Nations, and to consider plans of union. Even a cursory reading of the plan proposed by the congress reveals the importance of the frontier. The powers of the general council and the officers were, chiefly, the determination of peace and war with the Indians, the regulation of Indian trade, the purchase of Indian lands, and the creation and government of new settlements as a security against the Indians. It is evident that the unifying tendencies of the Revolutionary period were facilitated by the previous co-operation in the regulation of the frontier. In this connection may be mentioned the importance of the frontier, from that day to this, as a military training school, keeping alive the power of resistance to aggression, and developing the stalwart and rugged qualities of the frontiersman.

THE RANCHER'S FRONTIER.

It would not be possible in the limits of this paper to trace the other frontiers across the continent. Travellers of the eighteenth century found the "cowpens" among the canebrakes and peavine pastures of the South, and the "cow drivers" took their droves to Charleston, Philadelphia, and New York.[27] Travellers at the close of the War of 1812 met droves of more than a thousand cattle and swine from the interior of Ohio going to Pennsylvania to fatten for the Philadelphia market.[28] The ranges of the Great Plains, with ranch and cowboy and nomadic life, are things of yesterday and of today. The experience of the Carolina cowpens guided the ranchers of Texas. One element favoring the rapid extension of the rancher's frontier is the fact that in a remote country lacking transportation facilities the product must be in small bulk, or must be able to transport itself, and the cattle raiser could easily drive his product to market. The effect of these great ranches on the subsequent agrarian history of the localities in which they existed should be studied.

THE FARMER'S FRONTIER.

The maps of the census reports show an uneven advance of the farmer's frontier, with tongues of settlement pushed forward and with identifications of wilderness. In part this is due to Indian resistance, in part to the location of river valleys and passes, in part to the unequal force of the centers of frontier attraction. Among the important centers of attraction may be mentioned the following: fertile and favorably situated soils, salt springs, mines and army posts.

ARMY POSTS.

The frontier army post, serving to protect the settlers from the Indians, has also acted as a wedge to open the Indian country, and has been a nucleus for settlement.[29] In this connection mention should also be made of the government military and exploring expeditions in determining the lines of settlement. But all the more important expeditions were greatly indebted to the earliest pathmakers, the Indian guides, the traders and trappers, and the French voyageurs, who were inevitable parts of governmental expeditions from the days of Lewis and Clark.[30] Each expedition was an epitome of the previous factors in western advance.

SALT SPRINGS.

In an interesting monograph, Victor Hehn[31] has traced the effect of salt upon early European development, and has pointed out how it affected the lines of settlement and the form of administration. A similar study might be made for the salt springs of the United States. The early settlers were tied to the coast by the need of salt, without which they could not preserve their meats or live in comfort. Writing in 1752, Bishop Spangenburg says of a colony for which he was seeking lands in North Carolina, "They will require salt & other necessaries which they can neither manufacture nor raise. Either they must go to Charleston, which is 300 miles distant. . . . Or else they must go to Boling's Point in Virginia on a branch of the James & is also 300 miles from here. . . . Or else they must go down the Roanoke—I know not how many miles—where salt is brought up from the Cape Fear."[32] This may serve as a typical illustration. An annual pilgrimage to the coast for salt thus became essential. Taking flocks or furs and ginseng root, the early settlers sent their pack trains after seeding time each year to the coast.[33] This proved to be an important educational influence, since it was almost the only way in which the pioneer learned what was going on in the East. But when discovery was made of the salt springs of the Kanawha, and the Holston, and Kentucky, and central New York, the West began to be freed from dependence on the coast. It was in part the effect of finding these salt springs that enabled settlement to cross the mountains.

From the time the mountains rose between the pioneer and the seaboard, a new order of Americanism arose. The West and the East began to get out of touch of each other. The settlements from the sea to the mountains kept connection with the rear and had a certain solidarity. But the overmountain men grew more and more independent. The East took a narrow view of American advance, and nearly lost these men. Kentucky and Tennessee history bears abundant witness to the truth of this statement. The East began to try to hedge and limit westward expansion. Though Webster could declare that there were no Alleghanies in his politics, yet in politics in general they were a very solid factor.

LAND.

Good soils have been the most continuous attraction to the farmer's frontier. The land hunger of the Virginians drew them down the rivers into Carolina, in early colonial days; the search for soils took the Massachusetts men to Pennsylvania and to New York. The exploitation of the beasts took hunter and trader to the west, the exploitation of the grasses took the rancher west, and the exploitation of the virgin soil of the river valleys and prairies attracted the farmer. As the eastern lands were taken up migration flowed across them to the west. Daniel Boone, the great backwoodsman, who combined the occupations of hunter, trader, cattle raiser, farmer and surveyor,—learning, probably from the traders, of the fertility of the lands on the upper Yadkin, where the traders were wont to rest as they took their way to the Indians, left his Pennsylvania home with his father, and passed down the Great Valley road to that stream. Learning from a trader whose posts were on the Red River in Kentucky of its game and rich pastures, he pioneered the way for the farmers to that region. Thence he passed to the frontier of Missouri, where his settlement was long a landmark on the frontier. Here again he helped to open the way for civilization, finding salt licks, and trails, and land. His son was among the earliest trappers in the passes of the Rocky Mountains, and his party are said to have been the first to camp on the present site of Denver. His grandson, Col. A. J. Boone, of Colorado, was a power among the Indians of the Rocky Mountains, and was appointed an agent by the government. Kit Carson's mother was a Boone.[34] Thus this family epitomizes the backwoodsman's advance across the continent.

The farmer's advance came in a distinct series of waves. In Peck's *New Guide to the West*, published in Cincinnati in 1848, occurs this suggestive passage:

"Generally, in all the western settlements, three classes, like the waves of the ocean, have rolled one after the other. First, comes the pioneer, who depends for the subsistence of his family chiefly upon the natural growth of vegetation, called the 'range,' and the proceeds of hunting. His implements of agriculture are rude, chiefly of his own make, and his efforts directed mainly to a crop of corn and a 'truck patch.' The last is a rude garden for growing cabbage, beans, corn for roasting ears, cucumbers and potatoes. A log cabin, and, occasionally, a stable and corn-crib, and a field of a dozen acres, the timber girdled or 'deadened,' and fenced, are enough for his occupancy. It is quite immaterial whether he ever becomes the owner of the soil. He is the occupant for the time being, pays no rent, and feels as independent as the 'lord of the manor.' With a horse, cow, and one or two breeders of swine, he strikes into the woods with his family, and becomes the founder of a new county, or perhaps state. He builds his cabin, gathers around him a few other families of similar tastes and habits, and occupies till the range is somewhat subdued, and hunting a little precarious, or, which is more frequently the case, till neighbors crowd around, roads, bridges, and fields annoy him, and he lacks elbow room. The pre-emption law enables him to dispose of his cabin and corn-field to the next class of emigrants; and, to employ his own figures, he 'breaks for the high timber,' 'clears out for the New Purchase,' or migrates to Arkansas or Texas, to work the same process over.

"The next class of emigrants purchase the lands, add field to field, clear out the roads, throw rough bridges over the streams, put up hewn log houses, with glass windows and brick or stone chimneys, occasionally plant orchards, build mills, school-houses, court-houses, etc., and exhibit the picture and forms of plain, frugal, civilized life.

"Another wave rolls on. The men of capital and enterprise come. The settler is ready to sell out, and take the advantage of the rise in property—push farther into the interior and become, himself, a man of capital and enterprise in turn. The small village rises to a spacious town or city; substantial edifices of brick, extensive fields, orchards, gardens, colleges and churches are seen. Broadcloths, silks, leghorns, crapes, and all the refinements, luxuries, elegancies, frivolities and fashions are in vogue. Thus wave after wave is rolling westward:—the real *Eldorado* is still farther on.

"A portion of the two first classes remain stationary amidst the general movement, improve their habits and condition, and rise in the scale of society.

"The writer has traveled much amongst the first class—the real pioneers. He has lived many years in connection with the second grade; and now the third wave is sweeping over large districts of Indiana, Illinois and Missouri. Migration has become almost a habit in the West. Hundreds of men can be found, not over fifty years of age, who have settled for the fourth, fifth or sixth time on a new spot. To sell out and remove only a few hundred miles makes up a portion of the variety of backwoods life and manners."[35]

Omitting the pioneer farmer who moves from the love of adventure, the advance of the more steady farmer is easy to understand. Obviously the immigrant was attracted by the cheap lands of the frontier, and even the native farmer felt their influence strongly. Year by year the farmers who lived on soil, whose returns were diminished by unrotated crops, were offered the virgin soil of the frontier at nominal prices. Their growing families demanded more lands, and these were dear. The competition of the unexhausted, cheap and easily tilled prairie lands compelled the farmer either to go west and continue the exhaustion of the soil on a new frontier, or to adopt intensive culture. Thus the census of 1890 shows, in the northwest, many counties in which there is an absolute, or a relative, decrease of population. These states have been sending farmers to advance the frontier on the plains, and have themselves begun to turn to intensive farming and to manufacture. A decade before this, Ohio had shown the same transition stage. Thus the demand for land and the love of wilderness freedom drew the frontier ever onward.

Having now roughly outlined the various kinds of frontiers, and their modes of advance, chiefly from the point of view of the frontier itself, we may next inquire what were the influences on the East and on the Old World. A rapid enumeration of some of the more noteworthy effects is all that I have time for.

COMPOSITE NATIONALITY.

First, we note that the frontier promoted the formation of a composite nationality for the American people. The coast was preponderantly English, but the later tides of continental immigration flowed across to the free lands. This was the case from the early colonial days. The Scotch-Irish and the Palatine Germans, or "Pennsylvania Dutch," furnished the stock of the colonial frontier. With these peoples were also the freed indented servants, or redemptioners, who at the expiration of their time of service passed to the frontier. Governor Spottswood of Virginia writes in 1717, "The inhabitants of our frontiers are composed generally of such as have been transported hither as servants, and, being out of their time, settle themselves where land is to be taken up and that will produce the necessarys of life with little labour."[36] Very generally these redemptioners were of non-English stock. In the crucible of the frontier the immigrants were Americanized, liberated and fused into a mixed race, English in neither nationality or characteristics. The process has gone on from the early days to our own. Burke and other writers in the middle of the eighteenth century believed that Pennsylvania[37] was "threatened with the danger of being wholly foreign in language, manners, and perhaps even inclinations." The German and Scotch-Irish elements in the frontier of the South were only less great. In the middle of the present century the German element in Wisconsin was already so considerable that leading publicists looked to the creation of a German state out of the commonwealth by concentrating their colonization.[38] Such examples teach us to beware of misinterpreting the fact that there is a common English speech in American into a belief that the stock is also English.

INDUSTRIAL INDEPENDENCE.

In another way the advance of the frontier decreased our dependence on England. The coast, particularly of the South, lacked diversified industries, and was dependent on England for the bulk of its supplies. In the

South there was even a dependence on the Northern colonies for articles of food. Governor Glenn of South Carolina writes in the middle of the eighteenth century: "Our trade with New York and Philadelphia was of this sort, draining us of all the little money and bills we could gather from other places for their bread, flour, beer, hams, bacon, and other things of their produce, all which, except beer, our new townships begin to supply us with, which are settled with very industrious and thriving Germans. This no doubt diminishes the number of shipping and the appearance of our trade, but it is far from being a detriment to us."[39] Before long the frontier created a demand for merchants. As it retreated from the coast it became less and less possible for England to bring her supplies directly to the consumer's wharfs, and carry away staple crops, and staple crops began to give way to diversified agriculture for a time. The effect of this phase of the frontier action upon the northern section is perceived when we realize how the advance of the frontier aroused seaboard cities like Boston, New York, and Baltimore, to engage in rivalry for what Washington called "the extensive and valuable trade of a rising empire."

EFFECTS ON NATIONAL LEGISLATION.

The legislation which most developed the powers of the national government, and played the largest part in its activity, was conditioned on the frontier. Writers have discussed the subjects of tariff, land, and internal improvement, as pendants to the slavery question. But when American history comes to be rightly viewed it will be seen that the slavery question is an incident. In the period from the end of the first half of the present century to the close of the Civil War, slavery rose to primary but far from exclusive importance. But this does not justify Professor von Holst (to take an example) in treating our constitutional history in its formative period down to 1828 in a single volume, and giving six volumes to the history of slavery from 1828 to 1861, under the title of a *Constitutional History of the United States*. The growth of nationalism and the evolution of American political institutions were dependent on the advance of the frontier. Even so recent a writer as Rhodes, in his *History of the United States since the Compromise of 1850*, has treated the legislation called out by the western advance as incidental to the slavery struggle.

This is a wrong perspective. The pioneer needed the goods of the coast, and so the grand series of internal improvement and railroad legislation began, with potent nationalizing effects. But the West was not content with bringing the farm to the factory. Under the lead of Clay— "Harry of the West"—protective tariffs were passed, with the cry of bringing the factory to the farm.

THE PUBLIC DOMAIN.

The public domain has been a force of profound importance in the nationalization and development of the government. The effects of the struggle of the landed and the landless states, and of the Ordinance of 1787, need no discussion.[40] Administratively the frontier called out some of the highest and most vitalizing activities of the general government. The purchase of Louisiana was perhaps the constitutional turning-point in the history of the republic, inasmuch as it afforded both a new area for national legislation, and the occasion of the downfall of the policy of strict construction. But the purchase of Louisiana was called out by frontier needs and demands. As frontier states accrued to the Union, the national power grew. In a speech on the dedication of the Calhoun monument, Lamar explained: "In 1789 the states were the creators of the federal government; in 1861, the federal government was the creator of a large majority of the states."

When we consider the public domain from the point of view of the sale and disposal of the public lands, we are again brought face to face with the frontier. The policy of the United States in dealing with its lands is in sharp contrast with the European system of scientific administration. Efforts to make this domain a source of revenue, and to withhold it from emigrants in order that settlement might be compact, were in vain. The jealousy and the fears of the East were powerless in the face of the demands of the frontiersmen. John Quincy Adams was obliged to confess: "My own system of administration, which was to make the national domain the inexhaustible fund for progressive and unceasing internal improvement, has failed." The reason is obvious; systems of administration was not what the West demanded; it wanted land. Adams states the situation as follows: "The slave holders of the South have bought the cooperation of the western country by the bribe of the western lands, abandoning to the new western states their own proportion of the public property and aiding them in the design of grasping all the lands into their own hands. Thomas H. Benton was the author of this system, which he brought forward as a substitute for the American system of Mr. Clay and to supplant him as the leading statesman of the West. Mr. Clay, by his tariff compromise with Mr. Calhoun, abandoned his own American system. At the same time he brought forward a plan for distributing among all the states of the Union the proceeds of the sales of the public lands. His bill for that purpose passed both Houses of Congress, but was vetoed by President Jackson, who, in his annual message of December, 1832, formally recommended that all public lands should be gratuitously given away to individual adventurers and to the states in which the lands are situated."[41]

"No subject," said Henry Clay, "which has presented itself to the present, or perhaps any preceding, congress, is of greater magnitude than that of the public lands." When we consider the far-reaching effects of the government's land policy upon political, economic, and social aspects of American life, we are disposed to agree with him. But this legislation was framed under frontier influences, and under the lead of Western statesmen like Benton and Jackson. Said Senator Scott of Indiana in 1841: "I consider the pre-emption law merely declaratory of the custom or common law of the settlers."

NATIONAL TENDENCIES OF THE FRONTIER.

It is safe to say that the legislation with regard to land, tariff, and internal improvements—the American system of the nationalizing Whig party—was conditioned on frontier ideas and needs. But it was not merely in legislative action that the frontier worked against the sectionalism of the coast. The economic and social characteristics of the frontier worked against sectionalism. The men of the frontier had closer resemblances to the Middle region than to either of the other sections. Pennsylvania had been the seed-plot of frontier emigration, and, although she passed on her settlers along the Great Valley into the west of Virginia and the Carolinas, yet the industrial society of these Southern frontiersmen was always more like that of the Middle region than like that of the tide-water portion of the South, which later came to spread its industrial type throughout the South.

The Middle region, entered by New York harbor, was an open door to all Europe. The tide-water part of the South represented typical Englishmen, modified by a warm climate and servile labor, and living in baronial fashion on great plantations; New England stood for a special English movement—Puritanism. The Middle region was less English than the other sections. It had a wide mixture of nationalities, a varied society, the mixed town and county system of local government, a varied economic life, many religious sects. In short it was a region mediating between New England and the South, and the East and the West. It represented that composite nationality which the contemporary United States exhibits, that juxtaposition of non-English groups, occupying a valley or a little settlement, and presenting reflections of the map of Europe in their variety. It was democratic and non-sectional, if not national; "easy, tolerant and contented;" rooted strongly in material prosperity. It was typical of the modern United States. It was least sectional, not only because it lay between North and South, but also because with no barriers to shut out its frontiers from its settled region, and with a system of connecting waterways, the Middle region mediated between East and West as well as between North and South. Thus it became the typically American region. Even the New Englander, who was shut out from the frontier by the Middle region, tarrying in New York or Pennsylvania on his westward march, lost the acuteness of his sectionalism on the way.[42]

Until the spread of cotton culture into the interior gave homogeneity to the South, the western part of it showed tendencies to fall away from the faith of the fathers into internal improvement legislation and nationalism. In the Virginia convention of 1829–30, called to revise the constitution, Mr. Leigh, of Chesterfield, one of the tide-water counties, declared:

"One of the main causes of discontent which led to this convention, that which had the strongest influence in overcoming our veneration for the work of our fathers, which taught us to contemn the sentiments of Henry and Mason and Pendleton, which weaned us from our reverence for the constituted authorities of the state, was an overweening passion for internal improvement. I say this with perfect knowledge; for it has been avowed to me by gentlemen from the West over and over again. And let me tell the gentleman from Albermarle (Mr. Gordon) that it has been another principal object of those who set this ball of revolution in motion, to overturn the doctrine of state rights, of which Virginia has been the very pillar, and to remove the barrier she has interposed to the interference of the federal government in that same work of internal improvement, by so reorganizing the legislature that Virginia, too, may be hitched to the federal car."

It was this nationalizing tendency of the West that transformed the democracy of Jefferson into the national republicanism of Monroe and the democracy of Andrew Jackson. The West of the War of 1812, the West of Clay, and Benton, and Harrison, and Andrew Jackson, shut off by the Middle states and the mountains from the coast sections, had a solidarity of its own with national tendencies. On the tide of the Father of Waters, North and South met and mingled into a nation. Interstate migration went steadily on—a process of cross-fertilization of ideas and institutions. The fierce struggle of the sections over slavery on the western frontier does not diminish the truth of this statement; it proves the truth of it. Slavery was a sectional trait that would not down, but in the West it could not remain sectional. It was the greatest of frontiersmen who declared: "I believe this government cannot endure permanently half slave and half free. It will become all of one thing, or all of the other." Nothing works for nationalism like intercourse within the nation. Mobility of population is death to localism, and the western frontier worked irresistibly in unsettling population. The effects reached back from the frontier and affected profoundly the Atlantic coast, and even the Old World.

GROWTH OF DEMOCRACY.

But the most important effect of the frontier has been in the promotion of democracy here and in Europe. As has been pointed out, the frontier is productive of individualism. Complex society is precipitated by the wilderness into a kind of primitive organization based on the family. The tendency is anti-social. It produces antipathy to control, and particularly to any direct control. The tax-gatherer is viewed as a representative of oppression. Professor Osgood, in an able article,[43] has pointed out that the frontier conditions prevalent in the colonies are important factors in the explanation of the American revolution, where individual liberty was sometimes confused with absence of all effective government. The same conditions aid in explaining the difficulty of instituting a strong government in the period of the confederacy. The frontier individualism has from the beginning promoted democracy.

The frontier states that came into the Union in the first quarter of a century of its existence came in with democratic suffrage provisions, and had reactive effects of the highest importance upon the older states whose peoples were being attracted there. It was *western* New York that forced an extension of suffrage in the constitutional convention of that state in 1820; and it was *western* Virginia that compelled the tide-water region to put a more liberal suffrage provision in the constitution framed in 1830, and to give to the frontier region a more nearly proportionate representation with the tide-water aristocracy. The rise of democracy as an effective force in the nation came in with western preponderance under Jackson and William Henry Harrison, and it meant the triumph of the frontier—with all of its good and with all of its evil elements.[44] An interesting illustration of the tone of frontier democracy in 1830 comes from the same debates in the Virginia convention already referred to. A representative from western Virginia declared: "But, sir, it is not the increase of population in the West which this gentleman ought to fear. It is the energy which the mountain breeze and western habits impart to those emigrants. They are regenerated, politically I mean, sir. They soon become *working politicians;* and the difference, sir, between a *talking* and a *working* politician is immense. The Old Dominion has long been celebrated for producing great orators; the ablest metaphysicians in policy; men that can split hairs in all abstruse questions of political economy. But at home, or when they return from congress, they have negroes to fan them asleep. But a Pennsylvania, a New York, an Ohio, or a western

Virginia statesman, though far inferior in logic, metaphysics and rhetoric to an old Virginia statesman, has this advantage, that when he returns home he takes off his coat and takes hold of the plough. This gives him bone and muscle, sir, and preserves his republican principles pure and uncontaminated."

So long as free land exists, the opportunity for a competency exists, and economic power secures political power. But the democracy born of free land, strong in selfishness and individualism, intolerant of administrative experience and education, and pressing individual liberty beyond its proper bounds, has its dangers as well as its benefits. Individualism in America has allowed a laxity in regard to governmental affairs which has rendered possible the spoils system, and all the manifest evils that follow from the lack of a highly developed civic spirit. In this connection may be noted also the influence of frontier conditions in permitting lax business honor, inflated paper currency and wild-cat banking. The colonial and revolutionary frontier was the region whence emanated many of the worst forms of an evil currency.[45] The West in the War of 1812 repeated the phenomenon on the frontier of that day, while the speculation and wild-cat banking of the period of the crisis of 1837 occurred on the new frontier belt of the next tier of states. Thus each one of the periods of lax financial integrity coincides with periods when a new set of frontier communities had arisen, and coincides in area with these successive frontiers for the most part. The recent Populist agitation is a case in point. Many a state that now declines any connection with the tenets of the Populists, itself adhered to such ideas in an earlier stage of the development of the state. A primitive society can hardly be expected to show the intelligent appreciation of the complexity of business interests in a developed society. The continual recurrence of these areas of paper-money agitation is another evidence that the frontier can be isolated and studied as a factor in American history of the highest importance.[46]

ATTEMPTS TO CHECK AND REGULATE THE FRONTIER.

The East has always feared the result of an unregulated advance of the frontier, and has tried to check and guide it. The English authorities would have checked settlement at the headwaters of the Atlantic tributaries and allowed the "savages to enjoy their deserts in quiet lest the peltry trade should decrease." This called out Burke's splendid protest:

"If you stopped your grants, what would be the consequence? The people would occupy without grants. They have already so occupied in many places. You cannot station garrisons in every part of these deserts. If you drive the people from one place, they will carry on their annual tillage and remove with their flocks and herds to another. Many of the people in the back settlements are already little attached to particular situations. Already they have topped the Appalachian mountains. From thence they behold before them an immense plain, one vast, rich, level meadow; a square of five hundred miles. Over this they would wander without a possibility of restraint; they would change their manners with their habits of life; would soon forget a government by which they were disowned; would become hordes of English Tartars; and, pouring down upon your unfortified frontiers a fierce and irresistible cavalry, become masters of your governors and your counselors, your collectors and comptrollers, and of all the slaves that adhered to them. Such would, and in no long time must, be the effect of attempting to forbid as a crime, and to suppress as an evil, the command and blessing of Providence, 'Increase and Multiply.' Such would be the happy result of an endeavor to keep as a lair of wild beasts that earth which God, by an express charter, has given to the children of men."

But the English government was not alone in its desire to limit the advance of the frontier, and guide its destinies. Tide-water Virginia[47] and South Carolina[48] gerrymandered those colonies to ensure the dominance of the coast in their legislatures. Washington desired to settle a state at a time, in the Northwest; Jefferson would reserve from settlement the territory of his Louisiana purchase north of the 32d parallel, in order to offer it to the Indians in exchange for their settlements east of the Mississippi. "When we shall be full on this side," he writes, "we may lay off a range of states on the western bank from the head to the mouth, and so range after range, advancing compactly as we multiply." Madison went so far as to argue to the French minister that the United States had no interest in seeing population extend itself on the right bank of the Mississippi, but should rather fear it. When the Oregon question was under debate, in 1824, Smyth, of Virginia, would draw an unchangeable line for the limits of the United States at the outer limit of two tiers of states beyond the Mississippi, complaining that the seaboard states were being drained of the flower of their population by the bringing of too much land into market. Even Thomas Benton, the man of widest views of the destiny of the West, at this stage of his career declared that along the ridge of the Rocky Mountains "the western limits of the republic should be drawn, and the statue of the fabled god Terminus should be raised upon its highest peak, never to be thrown down."[49] But the attempts to limit our boundaries, to restrict land sales and settlement, and to deprive the West of its share of political power, were all in vain. Steadily that frontier of settlement advanced and carried with it individualism, democracy and nationalism, and powerfully affected the Old World.

MISSIONARY ACTIVITY.

The most effective efforts of the East to regulate the frontier came
through its educational and religious activity, exerted by interstate migration and by organized societies. Speaking in 1835, Dr. Lyman Beecher
declared: "It is equally plain that the religious and political destiny of our
nation is to be decided in the West," and he pointed out that the population of the West "is assembled from all the states of the Union, and from
all the nations of Europe, and is rushing in like the waters of the flood,
demanding for its moral preservation the immediate and universal action
of those institutions which discipline the mind and arm the conscience
and the heart. And so various are the opinions and habits, and so recent
and imperfect is the acquaintance, and so sparse are the settlements of
the West, that no homogeneous public sentiment can be formed to legis-
late immediately into being the requisite institutions. And yet they are all
needed immediately in their utmost perfection and power. A nation is
being 'born in a day'. . . But what will become of the West if her prosperity rushes up to such a majesty of power, while those great institutions
linger which are necessary to form the mind and the conscience, and the
heart of that vast world. It must not be permitted. . . . Let no man at the
East quiet himself and dream of liberty, whatever may become of the
West. . . . Her destiny is our destiny."[50]

With this appeal to the conscience of New England, he adds appeals
to her fears lest other religious sects anticipate her own. The New England preacher and school teacher left their mark on the West. The dread
of western emancipation from New England's political and economic
control was paralleled by fears lest the West cut loose from her religion.
Commenting in 1850 on reports that settlement was rapidly extending
northward in Wisconsin, the editor of *The Home Missionary* writes:
"We scarcely know whether to rejoice or to mourn over this extension of
our settlements. While we sympathize in whatever tends to increase the
physical resources and prosperity of our country, we cannot forget that
with all these dispersions into remote and still remoter corners of the
land, the supply of the means of grace is becoming relatively less and
less." Acting in accordance with such ideas, home missions were established and western colleges were erected. As seaboard cities like Philadelphia, New York and Baltimore strove for the mastery of western
trade, so the various denominations strove for the possession of the
West. Thus an intellectual stream from New England sources fertilized
the West. On the other hand, the contest for power and the expansive
tendency furnished to the various sects by the existence of a moving
frontier, must have had important results on the character of religious

organizations in the United States. It is a chapter in our history which needs study.

INTELLECTUAL TRAITS.

From the conditions of frontier life came intellectual traits of profound importance. The works of travellers along each frontier from colonial days onward describe for each certain traits, and these traits have, while softening down, still persisted as survivals in the place of their origin, even when a higher social organization succeeded. The result is that to the frontier the American intellect owes its striking characteristics. That coarseness and strength combined with acuteness and inquisitiveness, that practical, inventive turn of mind, quick to find expedients, that masterful grasp of material things, lacking in the artistic but powerful to effect great ends, that restless, nervous energy,[51] that dominant individualism, working for good and for evil, and withal that buoyancy and exuberance which comes with freedom,—these are traits of the frontier, or traits called out elsewhere because of the existence of the frontier. Since the days when the fleet of Columbus sailed into the waters of the New World, America has been another name for opportunity, and the people of the United States have taken their tone from the incessant expansion which has not only been open but has even been forced upon them. He would be a rash prophet who should assert that the expansive character of American life has now entirely ceased. Movement has been its dominant fact, and, unless this training has no effect upon a people, the American intellect will continually demand a wider field for its exercise. But never again will such gifts of free land offer themselves. For a moment at the frontier the bonds of custom are broken, and unrestraint is triumphant. There is not *tabula rasa*. The stubborn American environment is there with its imperious summons to accept its conditions; the inherited ways of doing things are also there; and yet, in spite of environment, and in spite of custom, each frontier did indeed furnish a new field of opportunity, a gate of escape from the bondage of the past; and freshness, and confidence, and scorn of older society, impatience of its restraints and its ideas, and indifference to its lessons, have accompanied the frontier. What the Mediterranean Sea was to the Greeks, breaking the bond of custom, offering new experiences, calling out new institutions and activities, that, and more, the ever retreating frontier has been to the United States directly, and to the nations of Europe more remotely. And now, four centuries from the discovery of America, at the end of a hundred years of life under the Constitution, the frontier has gone, and with its going has closed the first period of American history.

The Significance of History

Frederick Jackson Turner

◆

THE CONCEPTIONS OF HISTORY have been almost as numerous as the men who have written history. To Augustine Birrell history is a pageant; it is for the purpose of satisfying our curiosity. Under the touch of a literary artist the past is to become living again. Like another Prospero the historian waves his wand, and the deserted streets of Palmyra sound to the tread of artisan and officer, warrior gives battle to warrior, ruined towers rise by magic, and the whole busy life of generations that have long ago gone down to dust comes to life again in the pages of a book. The artistic prose narration of past events—this is the ideal of those who view history as literature. To this class belong romantic literary artists who strive to give to history the coloring and dramatic action of fiction, who do not hesitate to paint a character blacker or whiter than he really was, in order that the interest of the page may be increased, who force dull facts into vivacity, who create impressive situations, who, in short, strive to realize as an ideal the success of Walter Scott. It is of the historic Froude that Freeman says: "The most winning style, the choicest metaphors, the neatest phrases from foreign tongues would all be thrown away if they were devoted to proving that any two sides of a triangle are not always greater than the third side. When they are devoted to proving that a man cut off his wife's head one day and married her maid the next morning out of sheer love for his country, they win believers for the paradox." It is of the reader of this kind of history that Seeley writes: "To him, by some magic, parliamentary debates shall be always lively, officials always men of strongly marked, interesting character. There shall be nothing to remind him of the blue-book or the law book, nothing common or prosaic; but he shall sit as in a theater and gaze at splendid scenery and costume. He shall never be called upon to study or to judge, but only to imagine and enjoy. His reflections, as he reads, shall be precisely those of the novel reader; he shall ask: Is this character well drawn? is it really amusing? is the interest of the story well sustained, and does it rise properly toward the close?"

But after all these criticisms we may gladly admit that in itself an interesting style, even a picturesque manner of presentation, is not to be condemned, provided that truthfulness of substance rather than vivacity of style be the end sought. But granting that a man may be the possessor of a good style which he does not allow to run away with him, either in the interest of the artistic impulse or in the cause of party, still there remain differences as to the aim and method of history. To a whole school of writers, among whom we find some of the great historians of our time, history is the study of politics, that is, in the high signification given the word of Aristotle, as meaning all that concerns the activity of the state itself. "History is past politics and politics present history," says the great author of the *Norman Conquest.* Maurenbrecher of Leipzig speaks in no less certain tones: "The bloom of historical studies is the history of politics;" and Lorenz of Jena asserts: "The proper field of historical investigation, in the closer sense of the word, is politics." Says Seeley: "The modern historian works at the same task as Artistotle in his Politics." "To study history is to study not merely a narrative but at the same time certain theoretical studies." "To study history is to study problems." And thus a great circle of profound investigators, with true scientific method, have expounded the evolution of political institutions, studying their growth as the biologist might study see bud, blossom, and fruit." The results of these labors may be seen in such monumental works as those of Waitz on German institutions, Stubbs on English constitutional history, and Maine on early institutions.

There is another and an increasing class of historians to whom history is the study of the economic growth of the people, who aim to show that property, the distribution of wealth, the social conditions of the people, are the underlying and determining factors to be studied. This school, whose advance guard was led by Roscher, having already transformed orthodox political economy by its historical method, is now going on to rewrite history from the economic point of view. Perhaps the best English expression of the ideas of the school is to be found in Thorold Rogers' *Economic Interpretation of History.* He asserts truly that "very often the cause of great political events and great social movements is economical and has hitherto been undetected." So important does the fundamental principle of this school appear to me that I desire to quote from Mr. Rogers a specific illustration of this new historical method.

"In the twelfth and thirteenth centuries [he writes] there were numerous and well frequented routes from the markets of Hindustan to the

Western world, and for the conveyance of that Eastern produce which was so greatly desired as a seasoning to the coarse and often unwholesome diet of our forefathers. The principal ports to which this produce was conveyed were Seleucia (latterly called Licia) in the Levant, Trebizond, and the Black Sea, and Alexandria. From these ports this Eastern produce was collected mainly by the Venetian and Genoese traders and conveyed over the passes of the Alps to the upper Danube and the Rhine. Here it was a source of great wealth to the cities which we planted on these waterways, from Ratisbon and Nuremberg to Bruges and Antwerp. The stream of commerce was not deep nor broad, but it was singularly fertilizing, and everyone who has any knowledge of the only history worth knowing knows how important these cities were in the later Middle Ages.

"In the course of time, all but one of these routes had been blocked by the savages who desolated central Asia, and still desolate it. It was therefore the object of the most enterprising of the Western nations to get, if possible, in the rear of these destructive brigands, by discovering a long sea passage to Hindustan. All Eastern trade depended on the Egyptian road being kept open, and this remaining road was already threatened. The beginning of this discovery was the work of a Portuguese prince. The expedition of Columbus was an attempt to discover a passage to India over the Western sea. By a curious coincidence the Cape passage was doubled, and the new world discovered almost simultaneously.

"The discoveries were made none too soon. Selim I (1512–20), the sultan of Turkey, conquered Mesopotamia and the holy towns of Arabia, and annexed Egypt during his brief reign. This conquest blocked the only remaining road which the Old World knew. The thriving manufactures of Alexandria were at once destroyed. Egypt ceased to be the highway from Hindustan. I discovered that some cause must be at work which had hitherto been unsuspected in the sudden and enormous rise of prices in all Eastern products, at the close of the first quarter of the sixteenth century, and found that it must have come from the conquest of Egypt. The river of commerce was speedily dried up. The cities which had thriven on it were gradually ruined, at least so far as this source of their wealth was concerned, and the trade of the Danube and Rhine ceased. The Italian cities fell into rapid decay. The German nobles, who had got themselves incorporated among the burghers of the free cities, were impoverished, and betook themselves the obvious expedient of reimbursing their losses by the pillage of their tenants. Then came the Peasants' War, its ferocious incidents, its cruel suppression, and the development of those wild sects which disfigured and arrested the German Reformation. The battle of the Pyramids, in which Selim gained the sultanate of Egypt for the Osmanli Turks, brought loss and misery into thousands of homes where the event had never been heard of. It is such facts as these which the economic interpretation of history illustrates and expounds."

Viewed from this position, the past is filled with new meaning. The focal point of modern interest is the fourth estate, the great mass of the people. History has been a romance and a tragedy. In it we read the brilliant annals of the few. The intrigues of courts, knightly valor, palaces and pyramids, the loves of ladies, the songs of minstrels, and the chants from cathedrals pass like a pageant, or linger like a strain of music as we turn the pages. But history has its tragedy as well, which tells of the degraded tillers of the soil, toiling that others might dream, the slavery that rendered possible the "glory that was Greece," the serfdom into which decayed the "grandeur that was Rome"—these as well demand their annals. Far oftener than has yet been shown have these underlying economic facts affecting the breadwinners of the nation been the secret of the nation's rise or fall, by the side of which much that has passed as history is the merest frippery.

But I must not attempt to exhaust the list of the conceptions of history. To a large class of writers, represented by Hume, the field of historical writing is an arena, whereon are to be fought out present partisan debates. Whig is to struggle against Tory, and the party of the writer's choice is to be victorious at whatever cost to the truth. We do not lack these partisan historians in America. To Carlyle, the hero-worshipper, history is the stage on which a few great men play their parts. To Max Müller history is the exposition of the growth of religious ideas. To the moralist history is the text whereby to teach a lesson. To the metaphysician history is the fulfillment of a few primary laws.

Plainly we may make choice from among many ideals. If, now, we strive to reduce them to some kind of order, we find that in each age a different ideal of history has prevailed. To the savage history is the painted scalp, with its symbolic representations of the victims of his valor; or it is the legend of the gods and heroes of his race—attempts to explain the origin of things. Hence the vast body of mythologies, folklore, and legends, in which science, history, fiction, are all blended together, judgment and imagination inextricably confused. As time passes the artistic instinct comes in, and historical writing takes the form of the Iliad, or the Nibelungenlied. Still we have in these writings the reflection of the imaginative, credulous age that believed in the divinity of its heroes and wrote down what it believed. Artistic and critical faculty find expression in Herodotus, father of Greek history, and in Thucydides, the ideal Greek historian. Both write from the standpoint of an advanced

civilization and strive to present a real picture of the events and an explanation of the causes of the events. But Thucydides is a Greek; literature is
to him an art, and history a part of literature; and so it seems to him no
violation of historical truth to make his generals pronounce long orations
that were composed for them by the historian. Moreover, early men and
Greeks alone believed their own tribe or state to be the favored of the
gods: the rest of humanity was for the most part outside the range of
history.

To the medieval historian history was the annals of the monastery, or
the chronicle of court and camp.

In the nineteenth century a new ideal and method of history arose.
Philosophy prepared the way for it. Schelling taught the doctrine "that
the state is not in reality governed by laws of man's devising, but is a
part of the moral order of the universe, ruled by cosmic forces from
above." Herder proclaimed the doctrine of growth in human institutions.
He saw in history the development of given germs; religions were to be
studied by comparison and by tracing their origins from superstitions up
toward rational conceptions of God. Language, too, was no sudden creation, but a growth, and was to be studied as such; and so with political
institutions. Thus he paved the way for the study of comparative philol-
ogy, of mythology, and of political evolution. Wolf, applying Herder's
suggestions to the Iliad, found no single Homer as its author, but many.
This led to the critical study of the texts. Niebuhr applied this mode of
study to the Roman historians and proved their incorrectness. Livy's
history of early Rome became legend. Then Niebuhr tried to find the real
facts. He believed that, although the Romans had forgotten their own
history, still it was possible by starting with institutions of known reality
to construct their predecessors, as the botanist may infer bud from
flower. He would trace causes from effects. In other words, so strongly
did he believe in the growth of an institution according to fixed laws that
he believed he could reconstruct the past, reaching the real facts even by
means of the incorrect accounts of the Roman writers.

Although he carried his method too far, still it was the foundation of
the modern historical school. He strove to reconstruct old Rome as it
really was out of the original authorities that remained. By critical analysis and interpretation he attempted so to use these texts that the buried
truth should come to light. To skill as an antiquary he added great political insight—for Niebuhr was a practical statesman. It was his aim to
unite critical study of the materials with the interpretative skill of the
political expert, and this has been the aim of the new school of historians.
Leopold von Ranke applied this critical method to the study of modern
history. To him a document surviving from the past itself was of far

greater value than any amount of tradition regarding the past. To him the contemporary account, rightly used, was of far higher authority than the second-hand relation. And so he searched diligently in the musty archives of European courts, and the result of his labors and those of his scholars has been the rewriting of modern diplomatic and political history. Charters, correspondence, contemporary chronicles, inscriptions, these are the materials on which he and his disciples worked. To "tell things as they really were" was Ranke's ideal. But to him, also, history was primarily past politics.

Superficial and hasty as this review has been, I think you see that the historical study of the first half of the nineteenth century reflected the thought of that age. It was an age of political agitation and inquiry, as our own age still so largely is. It was an age of science. That inductive study of phenomena which has worked a revolution in our knowledge of the external world was applied to history. In a word, the study of history became scientific and political.

Today the questions that are uppermost and that will become increasingly important, are not so much political as economic questions. The age of machinery, of the factory system, is also the age of socialistic inquiry.

It is not strange that the predominant historical study is coming to be the study of past social conditions, inquiry as to landholding, distribution of wealth, and the economic basis of society in general. Our conclusion, therefore, is that there is much truth in all these conceptions of history: history is past literature, it is past politics, it is past religion, it is past economics.

Each age tries to form its own conception of the past. *Each age writes the history of the past anew with reference to the conditions uppermost in its own time.* Historians have accepted the doctrine of Herder. Society grows. They have accepted the doctrine of Comte. Society is an organism. History is the biography of society in all its departments. There is objective history and subjective history. Objective history applies to the events themselves; subjective history is man's conception of these events. "The whole mode and manner of looking at things alters with every age," but this does not mean that the real events of a given age change; it means that our comprehension of these facts changes.

History, both objective and subjective, is ever *becoming*, never completed. The centuries unfold to us more and more the meaning of past times. Today we understand Roman history better than did Livy or Tacitus, not only because we know how to use the sources better but also because the significance of events develops with time, because today is so much a product of yesterday that yesterday can only be understood as it is explained by today. The aim of history, then, is to know the elements of the present by understanding what came into the present from the past. For the present is simply the developing past, the past the undeveloped present. As well try to understand the egg without a knowledge of its developed form, the chick, as to try to understand the past without bringing to it the explanation of the present; and equally well try to understand an animal without study of its embryology as to understand one's time without study of the events that went before. The antiquarian strives to bring back the past for the sake of the past; the historian strives to show the present to itself by revealing its origin from the past. The goal of the antiquarian is the dead past; the goal of the historian is the living present. Droysen has put this true conception into the statement, "History is the 'Know Thyself' of humanity—the self-consciousness of mankind."

If, now, you accept with me the statement of this great master of historical science, the rest of our way is clear. If history be, in truth, the self-consciousness of humanity, the "self-consciousness of the living age, acquired by understanding its development from the past," all the rest follows.

First we recognize why all the spheres of man's activity must be considered. Not only is this the only way in which we can get a complete view of the society, but not one department of social life can be understood in isolation from the others. The economic life and the political life touch, modify, and condition one another. Even the religious life needs to be studied in conjunction with the political and economic life, and vice versa. Therefore all kinds of history are essential—history as politics, history as art, history as economics, history as religion—all are truly parts of society's endeavor to understand itself by understanding its past.

Next we see that history is not shut up in a book—not in many books. The first lesson the student of history has to learn is to discard his conception that there are standard ultimate histories. In the nature of the case this is impossible. *History is all the remains that have come down to us from the past, studied with all the critical and interpretative power that the present can bring to the task.* From time to time great masters bring their investigations to fruit in books. To us these serve as the latest words, the best results of the most recent efforts of society to understand itself—but they are not the final words. To the historian the materials for his work are found in all that remains from the ages gone by—in papers, roads, mounds, customs, languages; in monuments, coins, medals, names, titles, inscriptions, charters; in contemporary annals and chronicles; and, finally, in the secondary sources, or histories in the common acceptance of the term. Wherever there remains a chipped flint, a spearhead, a piece of pottery, a pyramid, a picture, a poem, a coliseum, or a coin, there is history.

Says Taine: "What is your first remark on turning over the great stiff leaves of a folio, the yellow sheets of a manuscript, a poem, a code of laws, a declaration of faith? This, you say, was not created alone. It is but a mold, like a fossil shell, an imprint like one of those shapes embossed in stone by an animal which lived and perished. Under the shell there was an animal, and behind the document there was a man. Why do you study the shell except to represent to yourself the animal? So do you study the document only in order to know the man. The shell and the document are lifeless wrecks, valuable only as a clue to the entire and living existence. We must reach back to this existence, endeavor to recreate it."

But observe that when a man writes a narration of the past he writes with all his limitations as regards ability to test the real value of his sources, and ability rightly to interpret them. Does he make use of a chronicle? First he must determine whether it is genuine; then whether it was contemporary, or at what period was written; then what opportunities its author had to know the truth; then what were his personal traits; was he likely to see clearly, to relate impartially? If not, what was his bias, what his limitations? Next comes the harder task—to interpret the significance of events; causes must be understood, results seen. Local affairs must be described in relation to affairs of the world—all must be told with just selection, emphasis, perspective; with that historical imagination and sympathy that does not judge the past by the canons of the present, nor read into it the ideas of the present. Above all the historian must have a passion for truth above that for any party or idea. Such are some of the difficulties that lie in the way of our science. When, moreover, we consider that each man is conditioned by the age in which he lives and must perforce write with limitations and prepossessions, I think we shall all agree that no historian can say the ultimate word.

Another thought that follows as a corollary from our definition is that in history there is a unity and a continuity. Strictly speaking, there is no gap between ancient, medieval, and modern history. Strictly speaking, there are no such divisions. Baron Bunsen dates modern history from the migration of Abraham. Bluntschli makes it begin with Frederick the Great. The truth is, as Freeman has shown, that the age of Pericles or the age of Augustus has more in common with modern times than has the age of Alfred or of Charlemagne. There is another test than that of chronology; namely, stages of growth. In the past of the European world peoples have grown from families into states, from peasantry into the complexity of great city life, from animism into monotheism, from mythology into philosophy; and have yielded place again to primitive peoples who in turn have passed through stages like these and yielded to new nations. Each nation has bequeathed something to its successor; no age has suffered the highest content of the past to be lost entirely. By unconscious inheritance and by conscious striving after the past as part of the present, history has acquired continuity. Freeman's statement that into Rome flowed all the ancient world and out of Rome came the modern world is as true as it is impressive. In a strict sense imperial Rome never died. You may find the eternal city still living in the Kaiser and the Czar, in the language of the Romance peoples, in the codes of European states, in the eagles of their coats of arms, in every college where the classics are read, in a thousand political institutions.

Even here in young America old Rome still lives. When the inaugural procession passes toward the Senate chamber, and the president's address outlines the policy he proposes to pursue, there is Rome! You may find her in the code of Louisiana, in the French and Spanish portions of our history, in the idea of checks and balances in our constitution. Clearest of all, Rome may be seen in the titles, government, and ceremonials of the Roman Catholic Church; for when the caesar passed away, his scepter fell to that new Pontiflex Maximus, the Pope, and to that new Augustus, the Holy Roman emperor of the Middle Ages, an empire which in name at least continued till those heroic times when a new Imperator recalled the days of the great Julius, and sent the eagles of France to proclaim that Napoleon was king over kings.

So it is true in fact, as we should presume a priori, that in history there are only artificial divisions. Society is an organism, ever growing. History is the self-consciousness of this organism. "The roots of the present lie deep in the past." There is no break. But not only is it true that no country can be understood without taking account of all the past; it is also true that we cannot select a stretch of land and say we will limit our study to this land; for local history can only be understood in the light of the history of the world. There is unity as well as continuity. To know the history of contemporary Italy we must know the history of contemporary France, of contemporary Germany. Each acts on each. Ideas, commodities even, refuse the bounds of a nation. All are inextricably connected, so that each is needed to explain the others. This is true especially of our modern world with its complex commerce and means of intellectual connection. In history, then, there is unity and continuity. Each age must be studied in the light of all the past; local history must be viewed in the light of world history.

Now, I think, we are in a position to consider the utility of historical studies. I will not dwell on the dignity of history considered as the self-consciousness of humanity; nor on the mental growth that comes from such a discipline; nor on the vastness of the field; all these occur to you, and their importance will impress you increasingly as you consider history from this point of view. To enable us to behold our own time and place as a part of the stupendous progress of the ages; to see primitive man; to recognize in our midst the undying ideas of Greece; to find Rome's majesty and power alive in present law and institution, still living in our superstitions and our folklore; to enable us to realize the richness of our inheritance, the possibility of our lives, the grandeur of the present—these are some of the priceless services of history.

But I must conclude my remarks with a few words upon the utility of history as affording a training for good citizenship. Doubtless good citizenship is the end for which the public schools exist. Were it otherwise there might be difficulty in justifying the support of them at public expense. The direct and important utility of the study of history in the achievement of this end hardly needs argument.

In the union of public service and historical study Germany has been pre-eminent. For certain governmental positions in that country a university training in historical studies is essential. Ex-President Andrew D. White affirms that a main cause of the efficiency of German administration is the training that officials get from the university study of history and politics. In Paris there is the famous School of Political Sciences which fits men for the public service of France. In the decade closing with 1887 competitive examinations showed the advantages of this training. Of sixty candidates appointed to the council of state, forty were graduates of this school. Of forty-two appointed to the inspection of finance, thirty-nine were from the school; sixteen of seventeen appointees to the court of claims; and twenty of twenty-six appointees to the department of foreign affairs held diplomas from the School of Political Sciences. In these European countries not merely are the departmental officers required to possess historical training; the list of leading statesmen reveals many names eminent in historical science. I need hardly recall to you the great names of Niebuhr the councilor whose history of Rome gave the impetus to our new science; of Stein, the reconstructor of Germany and the projector of the Monumenta Germanicae, that priceless collection of original sources of medieval history. Read the roll of Germany's great public servants and you will find among them such eminent men as Gneist, the authority on English constitutional history; Bluntschli, the able historian of politics; Von Holst, the historian of our own political development; Knies, Roscher, and Wagner, the economists; and many more. I have given you Droysen's conception of history. But Droysen was not simply a historian; he belonged, with the famous historians Treitschke, Mommsen, Von Sybel, to what Lord Acton calls "that central band of writers and statesmen and soldiers who turned the tide that had run for six hundred years, and conquered the centrifugal forces that had reigned in Germany longer than the commons have sat at Westminster."

Nor does England fail to recognize the value of the union of history and politics, as is exemplified by such men as Macaulay, Dilke, Morley, and Bryce, all of whom have been eminent members of Parliament as well as distinguished historical writers. From France and Italy such illustrations could easily be multiplied.

When we turn to America and ask what marriages have occurred between history and statesmanship, we are filled with astonishment at the contrast. It is true that our country has tried to reward literary men; Motley, Irving, Bancroft, Lowell held official positions, but these positions were in the diplomatic service. The "literary fellow" was good enough for Europe. The state gave these men aid rather than called their services to its aid. To this statement I know of but one important exception—George Bancroft. In America statesmanship has been considered something of spontaneous generation, a miraculous birth from our republican institutions. To demand of the statesmen who debate such topics as the tariff, European and South American relations, immigration, labor and railroad problems, a scientific acquaintance with historical politics or economics would be to expose one's self to ridicule in the eyes of the public. I have said that the tribal stage of society demands tribal history and tribal politics. When a society is isolated it looks with contempt upon the history and institutions of the rest of the world. We shall not be altogether wrong if we say that such tribal ideas concerning our institutions and society have prevailed for many years in this country. Lately historians have turned to the comparative and historical study of our political institutions. The actual working of our constitution as contrasted with the literary theory of it has engaged the attention of able young men. Foreigners like Von Holst and Bryce have shown us a mirror of our political life in the light of the political life of other peoples. Little of this influence has yet attracted the attention of our public men. Count the roll in Senate and House, cabinet and diplomatic service—to say nothing of the state governments—and where are the names famous in history and politics? It is shallow to express satisfaction with this condition and to sneer at "literary fellows." To me it seems that we are approaching a pivotal point in our country's history.

In an earlier part of my remarks I quoted from Thorold Rogers to show how the Turkish conquest of far-off Egypt brought ruin to homes in Antwerp and Bruges. If this was true in that early day, when commercial threads were infinitely less complex than they are now, how profoundly is our present life interlocked with the events of all the world?

Heretofore America has remained aloof from the Old World affairs. Under the influence of a wise policy she has avoided political relations with other powers. But it is one of the profoundest lessons that history has to teach, that political relations, in a highly developed civilization, are inextricably connected with economic relations. Already there are signs of a relaxation of our policy of commercial isolation. Reciprocity is a word that meets with increasing favor from all parties. But once fully afloat on the sea of worldwide economic interests, we shall soon develop political interests. Our fishery disputes furnish one example; our Samoan interests another; our Congo relations a third. But perhaps most important are our present and future relations with South America, coupled with our Monroe Doctrine. It is a settled maxim of international law that the government of a foreign state whose subjects have lent money to another state may interfere to protect the rights of the bondholder, if they are endangered by the borrowing state. As Professor H. B. Adams has pointed out, South American states have close financial relations with many European money-lenders; they are also prone to revolutions. Suppose, now, that England, finding the interests of her bondholders in jeopardy, should step in to manage the affairs of some South American country as she has those of Egypt for the same reason. Would the United States abandon its popular interpretation of the Monroe Doctrine, or would she give up her policy of noninterference in the political affairs of the outer world? Or suppose our own bondholders in New York, say, to be in danger of loss from revolution in South America—and our increasing tendency to close connection with South American affairs makes this a supposable case—would our government stand idly by while her citizens' interests were sacrificed? Take another case, the protectorate of the proposed interoceanic canal. England will not be content to allow the control of this to rest solely in our hands. Will the United States form an alliance with England for the purpose of this protection? Such questions as these indicate that we are drifting out into European political relations, and that a new statesmanship is demanded, a statesmanship that shall clearly understand European history and present relations, which depend on history.

Again, consider the problems of socialism brought to our shores by European immigrants. We shall never deal rightly with such problems until we understand the historical conditions under which they grew. Thus we meet Europe not only outside our borders but in our very midst. The problem of immigration furnishes many examples of the need of historical study. Consider how our vast Western domain has been settled. Louis XIV devastates the Palatinate, and soon hundreds of its inhabitants are hewing down the forests of Pennsylvania. The bishop of

Salzburg persecutes his Protestant subjects, and the woods of Georgia sound to the crack of Teutonic rifles. Presbyterians are oppressed in Ireland, and soon in Tennessee and Kentucky the fires of pioneers gleam. These were but advance guards of the mighty army that has poured into our midst ever since. Every economic change, every political change, every military conscription, every socialistic agitation in Europe, has sent us groups of colonists who have passed out onto our prairies to form new self-governing communities, or who have entered the life of our great cities. These men have come to us historical products, they have brought to us not merely so much bone and sinew, not merely so much money, not merely so much manual skill, they have brought with them deeply inrooted customs and ideas. They are important factors in the political and economic life of the nation. Our destiny is interwoven with theirs; how shall we understand American history without understanding European history? The story of the peopling of America has not yet been written. We do not understand ourselves.

One of the most fruitful fields of study in our country has been the process of growth of our own institutions, local and national. The town and the county, the germs of our political institutions, have been traced back to old Teutonic roots. Gladstone's remark that "the American constitution is the most wonderful work ever struck off at a given time by the brain and purpose of man" has been shown to be misleading, for the constitution was, with all the constructive powers of the fathers, still a growth; and our history is only to be understood as a growth from European history under the new conditions of the New World.

Says Dr. H. B. Adams: "American local history should be studied as a contribution to national history. This country will yet be viewed and reviewed as an organism of historic growth, developing from minute germs, from the very protoplasm of state-life. And some day this country will be studied in its international relations, as an organic part of a larger organism now vaguely called the World-State, but as surely developing through the operation of economic, legal, social, and scientific forces as the American Union, the German and British empires are evolving into higher forms.... The local consciousness must be expanded into a fuller sense of its historic worth and dignity. We must understand the cosmopolitan relations of modern local life, and its own wholesome conservative power in these days of growing centralization."

If any added argument were needed to show that good citizenship demands the careful study of history, it is in the examples and lessons that the history of other peoples has for us. It is profoundly true that each people makes its own history in accordance with its past. It is true that a purely artificial piece of legislation, unrelated to present and past conditions, is the most short-lived of things. Yet it is to be remembered that it was history that taught us this truth, and that there is, within the limits of the constructive action possible to a state, large scope for the use of this experience of foreign peoples.

I have aimed to offer, then, these considerations: History, I have said, is to be taken in no narrow sense. It is more than past literature, more than past politics, more than past economics. It is the self-consciousness of humanity—humanity's effort to understand itself through the study of its past. Therefore it is not confined to books; the subject is to be studied, not books simply. History has a unity and a continuity; the present needs the past to explain it; and local history must be read as a part of world history. The study has a utility as a mental discipline, and as expanding our ideas regarding the dignity of the present. But perhaps its most practical utility to us, as public school teachers, is its service in fostering good citizenship.

The ideals presented may at first be discouraging. Even to him who devotes his life to the study of history the ideal conception is impossible of attainment. He must select some field and till that thoroughly, be absolute master of it; for the rest he must seek the aid of others whose lives have been given in the true scientific spirit to the study of special fields. The public school teacher must do the best with the libraries at this disposal. We teachers must use all the resources we can obtain and not pin our faith to a single book; we must make history living instead of allowing it to seem mere literature, a mere narration of events that might have occurred on the moon. We must teach the history of a few countries thoroughly, rather than that of many countries superficially. The popularizing of scientific knowledge is one of the best achievements of this age of book-making. It is typical of that social impulse which has led university men to bring the fruits of their study home to the people. In England the social impulse has led to what is known as the university extension movement. University men have left their traditional cloister and gone to live among the working classes, in order to bring to them a new intellectual life. Chautauqua, in our own country, has begun to pass beyond the period of superficial work to a real union of the scientific and the popular. In their summer school they offer courses in American history. Our own state university carries on extensive work in various lines. I believe that this movement in the direction of popularizing historical and scientific knowledge will work a real revolution in our towns and villages as well as in our great cities.

The school teacher is called to do a work above and beyond the instruction in his school. He is called upon to be the apostle of the higher culture to the community in which he is placed. Given a good school or town library—such a one is now within the reach of every hamlet that is properly stimulated to the acquisition of one—and given an energetic, devoted teacher to direct and foster the study of history and politics and economics, we would have an intellectual regeneration of the state. Historical study has for its end to let the community see itself in the light of the past, to give it new thoughts and feelings, new aspirations and energies. Thought and feelings flow into deeds. Here is the motive power that lies behind institutions. This is therefore one of the ways to create good politics; here we can touch the very "age and body of the time, its form and pressure." Have you a thought of better things, a reform to accomplish? "Put it in the air," says the great teacher. Ideas have ruled, will rule. We must make university extension into state life felt in this country as did Germany. Of one thing beware. Avoid as the very unpardonable sin any one-sidedness, any partisan, any partial treatment of history. Do not misinterpret the past for the sake of the present. The man who enters the temple of history must respond devoutly to that invocation of the church, *Sursum corda*, lift up your hearts. No looking at history as an idle tale, a compend of anecdotes; no servile devotion to a textbook; no carelessness of truth about the dead that can no longer speak must be permitted in its sanctuary. "History," says Droysen, "is not the truth and the light; but a striving for it, a sermon on it, a consecration to it."

BIBLIOGRAPHICAL NOTE

In the preparation of this lecture free use has been made of the following sources: notes on the lectures of Professor Herbert B. Adams of Johns Hopkins University; J. Cotter Morrison, "History," in the *Encyclopaedia Britannica*; Augustine Birrell, "The Muse of History," in the *Contemporary Review* (London), 47:770–80 (June, 1885); Edward A. Freeman, *Methods of Historical Study* (London, 1886); John R. Seeley, "History and Politics," in *Macmillan's Magazine* (New York), 40:289–99, 369–78, 449–58 (August–October, 1879), and "On History Again," 47:67 (November, 1882); Charles K. Adams, *Manual of Historical Literature* (New York, 1889), Preface; Elisha B. Andrews, *Brief Institutes of General History* (3d edition, Boston, 1891), ch.1; Lord Acton, "German Schools of History," in the *English Historical Review* (London and New York), 1:7–42 (January, 1886); Ernst Bernheim, *Lehrbuch der historischen Methode* (Leipzig, 1889) and *Geschichtsforschung und Geschichtsphilosophie* (Gottingen, 1880); Wilhelm Maurenbrecher, *Uber Methode und Aufgabe der historischen Forschung* (Bonn, 1868) and *Geschichte und Politik* (Leipzig, 1884); Ottokar Lorenz, *Die Geschichtswissenschaft in Hauptrichtungen und Aufgaben* (Berlin, 1886); R. Rocholl, *Die Philosophieder Geschichte* (2 vols., Gottingen, 1878, 1893); and Johann G. Droysen, *Grundriss der Historik* (2d edition, Leipzig, 1875).

Bibliographic Note

James P. Danky

◆

TOO FREQUENTLY, it seems, the importance of a particular creative work is not recognized at the time of its creation. The classic example of not recognizing the important among the mundane would, of course, be Lincoln's Gettysburg Address. When Lincoln said, "The world will little note, nor long remember, what we say here," he was quite correct in assessing the public memory of what the *other* speakers said on that November day in 1863. That this should be so is self-evident to anyone who has been in the audience during a lengthy presentation of academic papers. As Martin Ridge notes, this was indeed the fate of Frederick Jackson Turner's address in Chicago in the summer of 1893 before the American Historical Association. (A namesake of the principal speaker at Gettysburg, Edward Everett, was among the history professors around the country to whom Turner sent copies of his essay thirty years later.)

Exactly six months after his Chicago appearance, Turner read "The Significance of the Frontier in American History" before the annual meeting of the State Historical Society of Wisconsin in Madison. His presentation in Chicago had been coupled with such other papers as "English Popular Uprisings in the Middle Ages," by Dr. George Kriehn, and by the Society's own Reuben Gold Thwaites's paper, "Early Lead Mining in Illinois and Wisconsin." Likewise, at the Madison meeting in December, Turner was joined by four others. According to the *Proceedings of the State Historical Society of Wisconsin*, Turner was the second speaker. The others were James Davie Butler, a clergyman, professor, author, and lecturer who discussed "Prehistoric Pottery—Middle Mississippi Valley"; Florence Elizabeth Baker, head of the Society's reading room for many years, who offered "A Brief History of the Elective Franchise in Wisconsin"; Matthew Brown Hammon, a well-known economist and governmental advisor, who presented "The Financial History of Wisconsin Territory"; and "Copper Currency in Louisiana in Colonial Times (1721–1726)," by Alexander John Gustavus Devron, a New Orleans physician and amateur historian. All of these essays, plus the financial reports, lists of library acquisitions, and other accounts of activities, were published in 1894. This was the forty-first such meeting of the Society, and the published proceedings served not only to document and publicize the work of the Society but were also a medium of exchange with other libraries and learned societies around the world. In addition to the full proceedings, the Society also published Turner's essay separately in 1894, a common practice both then and now.

The first discrete publication of *The Significance of the Frontier in American History* is a separately paged pamphlet on an inexpensive paper common at the time. The thirty-four pages, enclosed in a plain gray cover, did not seem destined to rescue Turner's essay from obscurity. But gradually the ideas that Turner set forth took root among his students and colleagues in the historical profession, and fifty years later, when Frederick B. Adams, Jr., Tom Streeter, and Carroll Wilson, New York book collectors, formed the committee for a Grolier Club exhibition, they selected his work. The committee's task was to select books that had influenced the life, culture, government, and literature of the United States. *One Hundred Influential American Books Printed Before 1900, Catalogue and Addresses; Exhibition at The Grolier Club April eighteenth–June sixteenth, 1946* (New York, The Grolier Club, 1947) includes Turner's modest pamphlet among *Moby-Dick*, the Bay Colony *Psalm Book*, Tom Paine's *Common Sense*, Whitman's *Leaves of Grass*, and other landmarks of American letters. After the agony of selection, the committee began the search for copies of the works for exhibition, some of which existed in understandably limited numbers. Only two copies of Parson Weems's *Washington* were extant, for example. But the committee had an especially difficult time locating a copy of Turner's *The Significance of the Frontier in American History*. As Adams notes in his introductory remarks, "This is a modern pamphlet, but it seems to have suffered a fate worse than a much older publication of a similar nature."

In 1977 the Library of Congress mounted a small but select exhibit drawn from its rare book collections. The accompanying publication, *Fifty Years of the Rare Book and Special Collections Division, An Exhibit Marking the 50th Anniversary of the Establishment of a Separate Rare Book Facility at the Library of Congress*, was intended to show the "fruits of fifty years of collecting" and not merely to show off valuable books. The exhibit reveals the generosity of donors to the Library of Congress and includes fifteenth-century manuscripts as well as Sigmund Freud's first book. Among the thirty-three selections is Turner's *The Sig-*

nificance of the Frontier in American History. The display copy was the State Historical Society's pamphlet, from the collection of Woodrow Wilson. It was inscribed by Turner to his former teacher and friend.

The Grolier Club and Library of Congress exhibitions are just some of the more noteworthy accolades that Turner's essay has received in the ninety years since he delivered it. The text of his remarks began to be widely reprinted soon after its public offering in 1893. The American Historical Society's *Annual Report* for 1893 included Turner's essay because of the Society's sponsorship of the Chicago meeting; it was issued both as a separate pamphlet and as part of the combined volume of the proceedings. *The Fifth Yearbook of the National Herbart Society for the Scientific Study of Teaching* printed the essay in 1899, thus making it available to the schoolteachers that Turner had often sought to reach. It also appeared in *The International Socialist Review* in December, 1905—the latter an odd choice for the conservative professor of history. From British and Canadian editions, inclusion in countless anthologies for secondary and college students, to translations such as *La Frontera en la historia Americana* (1961), Turner's words persist. *The Frontier in American History*, a collection of Turner's essays and one of the few books produced by him in his lifetime, was reissued in 1986 by the University of Arizona Press with a foreword by Wilbur R. Jacobs. Among the most beautiful printings of his famous essay is the Cornell University Press edition (1956) with woodcuts by Elfriede Abbe. In 1984 the Silver Buckle Press of the University of Wisconsin–Madison, with the assistance of the State Historical Society of Wisconsin, published a limited edition of Turner's essay which was prefaced by the words of Martin Ridge. The first copy of the edition was presented in April, 1985, to Merle Curti, last living member of Turner's seminar and, like Turner, the winner of a Pulitzer Prize in history.

The State Historical Society of Wisconsin was intimately involved with Frederick Jackson Turner from the beginning. The richness of the collections at the Society, gathered by Lyman C. Draper, Daniel Durrie, and Reuben G. Thwaites, provided the sources in which Turner grounded and tested his ideas. The provision of an office for Professor Turner was but one of many examples of the close relationship between the great university and its equally celebrated library.

The State Historical Society of Wisconsin is the oldest scholarly publisher in Wisconsin. It has published many other important works during the past hundred and twenty-five years, including Turner's "The Significance of the Section in American History" in the *Wisconsin Magazine of History*. None of these compares in influence or fame to the thirty-four-page pamphlet containing Frederick Jackson Turner's seminal essay.

NOTES TO THE TEXT

INTRODUCTION

[1]See Martin Ridge, "A More Jealous Mistress: Frederick Jackson Turner as Book Reviewer," in the *Pacific Historical Review*, 55:49–63 (February, 1986).

[2]Vernon E. Mattson and William E. Marion, *Frederick Jackson Turner: A Reference Guide* (Boston, 1985).

[3]Ray Allen Billington, *Frederick Jackson Turner: Historian, Scholar, Teacher* (New York, 1973). See also Martin Ridge, "Ray Allen Billington (1903–1981)," in the *Western Historical Quarterly*, 12:245–250 (July, 1981).

[4]Ray Allen Billington, *Westward Expansion: A History of the American Frontier* (New York, 1949), vii–viii.

[5]Ray Allen Billington, *The Genesis of the Frontier Thesis: A Study in Historical Creativity* (San Marino, California, 1971); and Ray Allen Billington, "On the Use of Manuscripts: A Confession," in the *Huntington Spectator* (Summer, 1979), 1–2.

[6]Ray Allen Billington, *American's Frontier Heritage* (New York, 1966).

[7]See Billington, *Genesis of the Frontier Thesis*.

[8]For example, see Norman Foerster, "American Literature," in the *Saturday Review of Literature*, 2:677–679 (April 3, 1926).

[9]Frederick Jackson Turner, *The Frontier in American History* (New York, 1920).

[10]For a sophisticated analysis of Turner's views on sectionalism and their importance, see Michael C. Steiner, "The Significance of Turner's Sectional Thesis," in the *Western Historical Quarterly*, 10:437–466 (October, 1979).

[11]For a convenient summary, see George Rogers Taylor, *The Turner Thesis: Concerning the Role of the Frontier in American History* (3rd edition, Lexington, Massachusetts, 1972).

[12]Ronald H. Carpenter, *The Eloquence of Frederick Jackson Turner* (San Marino, California, 1983).

[13]Turner, *The Frontier in American History*, 269–289.

YOUNG FRED TURNER

[1]A sketch of Andrew Jackson Turner's life, apparently from his own pen, is in *A History of Columbia County* (Chicago, 1880), 930–931. His newspaper career is emphasized in Fulmer Mood, "Frederick Jackson Turner and the Milwaukee *Sentinel*, 1884," in the *Wisconsin Magazine of History*, 34:21–28 (Autumn, 1959), and his political activity in Donald J. Berthrong, "Andrew Jackson Turner, Workhorse of the Republican Party," also in the *Wisconsin Magazine of History*, 38:77–86 (Winter, 1954).

[2]"Notes for Talk to Harvard History Club, 1924," Frederick Jackson Turner Papers, Henry E. Huntington Library, TU 56. (Hereinafter cited as Turner Papers, HEH.)

[3]Frederick Jackson Turner to Joseph Schafer, October 14, 1931, Turner Papers, HEH, TU Box 45.

[4]Turner to Carl Becker, December 16, 1925, Turner Papers, HEH, TU Box 34.

[5]Turner to Caroline Mae Sherwood, May 20, 1888, Turner Papers, HEH, TU Box A.

[6]Turner to Mrs. William Hooper, February 13, 1921, Turner Papers, HEH, TU-H Box 5.

[7]Turner to Carl Becker, December 16, 1925, Turner Papers, HEH, TU Box 34. For a similar instance of Turner's memory of the racial groups in Columbia County, see Turner to Constance L. Skinner, March 15, 1922, Turner Papers, HEH, TU Box 31. This letter has been printed by Constance L. Skinner as "Turner's Autobiographical Letter," in the *Wisconsin Magazine of History*, 19:91–103 (September, 1935).

[8]Reminiscences of Amplius Chamberlain in *History of Columbia County*, 439. For an account of earlier settlements at Portage, see *ibid.*, 588–589.

[9]*Ibid.*, 330–333, 364–365.

[10]Construction of the canal was begun in 1837 by the Portage Canal Company, which soon languished for want of capital. Work was resumed in 1849 under stimulus of the land grant, and the

canal briefly opened in 1851, but high water soon washed away most of the improvements. An enlarged land grant in 1854 and 1855 again stimulated interest, but a workable canal was not opened until 1874, and then as a project of the United States government. *Ibid.*, 610–612.

[11]*Ibid.*, 182–183, 486–493; William F. Raney, *Wisconsin: A Story of Progress* (New York, 1940), 192–193. Turner's father's role as a railroad promoter is discussed in Berthrong, "Andrew Jackson Turner," WMH, 38:84–85.

[12]Milo M. Quaife, *Wisconsin; Its History and Its People* (4 vols., Chicago, 1924), I:528; James S. Ritchie, *Wisconsin and Its Resources* (3rd ed., Chicago, 1858) 132.

[13]*History of Columbia County*, 589–592.

[14]*Ibid.*, 591.

[15]*Population of the United States in 1860; Compiled from the Original Returns of the Eighth Census* (Washington, 1864), 543; *History of Columbia County*, 454, 599, 606; 633–637; John W. Hunt, *Wisconsin Gazetteer* (Madison, 1853), 177–178.

[16]Loa K. Mauisolff to Turner, November 10, 1929, Turner Papers, HEH, TU Box 1.

[17]This address is printed in part in Mood, "Frederick Jackson Turner and the Milwaukee *Sentinel*", WMH, 34:23. Turner's high school diploma, dated June 28, 1878, is in the Turner Papers, HEH, TU Box 53; a copy of the graduation program is in *ibid.*, Box B. A list of members of the graduating class is in *History of Columbia County*, 623–624.

[18]*History of Columbia County*, 655–656, lists members of the company in 1880. Turner's father was its president at that time. The company was named after its sponsor, Joshua J. Guppey.

[19]*Statistics of the Population of the United States at the Tenth Census (June 1, 1880)*, Vol. I (Washington, 1883), 367, 425, 456.

[20]*History of Columbia County*, 494–495. William H. Spain was the attorney for Patrick Wildrick, a habitual criminal. See Richard N. Current, *The History of Wisconsin. Volume II: The Civil War Era, 1848–1873* (Madison, 1976), 523–527.

[21]*Ibid.*, 186; Raney, *Wisconsin*, 209–215; A. G. Ellis, "The 'Upper Wisconsin' Country," in *Third Annual Report and Collections of the State Historical Society of Wisconsin for the Year 1856* (Madison, 1857), 441–444. The latter contains an excellent contemporary account of rafting near Portage.

[22]Turner to Caroline Mae Sherwood, August 1886, Turner Papers, HEH, TU Box A.

[23]*Population of the United States in 1860*, 527; *Statistics of the Population of the United States at the Tenth Census*, 414, 446, 534, 535.

[24]Brief descriptions of these towns are in *History of Columbia County*, 497–498, 706. Montello village had a population of 395 in 1880. See *Statistics of Population of the United States at the Tenth Census*, 370.

[25]Turner to Caroline Mae Sherwood, July 19, 1886, Turner Papers, HEH, TU Box A.

[26]Turner to Caroline Mae Sherwood, July 15, 1888, Turner Papers, HEH, TU, Box A.

[27]Turner to Luther L. Bernard, November 24, 1928, Turner Papers, HEH, TU, Box 40.

[28]Turner to Helen Solliday, May 27, 1930, Turner Papers, HEH, TU Box 44.

[29]Turner to Caroline Mae Sherwood [1887], Turner Papers, HEH, TU Box A.

[30]Turner to Andrew Jackson Turner, September 23, 1885, Turner Papers, HEH, TU Box B.

[31]Turner's essay on the Grignon tract was originally in the Portage *Wisconsin State Register*, June 23, 1883. It has been reprinted, with an excellent scholarly introduction, in Fulmer Mood and Everett E. Edwards, "Frederick Jackson Turner's History of the Grignon Tract on the Portage of the Fox and Wisconsin Rivers," in *Agricultural History*, 17:113–120 (April, 1943).

[32]Commonplace Book, II, Turner Papers, HEH, TU Vol. III.

[33]Commonplace Book, I, Turner Papers, HEH, TU Vol. III.

[34]Commonplace Book, II, Turner Papers, HEH, TU Vol. III.

[35]Turner to William Francis Allen, July 11, 1888, Frederick Jackson Turner Papers, State Historical Society of Wisconsin, Box 2.

[36]Turner to William Francis Allen [January, 1889?], Turner Papers, HEH, TU Box 1.

[37]*Ibid.*

THE SIGNIFICANCE OF THE FRONTIER

[1]The foundation of this paper is my article entitled, "Problems in American History," which appeared in *The Aegis*, a publication of the students of the University of Wisconsin, November 8,

1892. This address was first delivered at a meeting of the American Historical Association, in Chicago, July 12, 1893. It is gratifying to find that Professor Woodrow Wilson—whose volume on "Division and Reunion," in the *Epochs of American History* series, has an appreciative estimate of the importance of the West as a factor in American history—accepts some of the views set forth in the papers above mentioned, and enhances their value by his lucid and suggestive treatment of them in his article in *The Forum*, December, 1893, reviewing Goldwin Smith's *History of the United States*.

[2]*Extra Census Bulletin*, No. 2, April 20, 1892.

[3]*Abridgment of Debates of Congress*, v, p. 706.

[4]*Bancroft* (1860 ed.), iii, pp. 344, 345, citing Logan MSS.; [Mitchell] *Contest in America*, etc. (1752), p. 237.

[5]Kercheval, *History of the Valley*; Bernheim, *German Settlements in the Carolinas*; Winsor, *Narrative and Critical History of America*, v, p. 304; *Colonial Records of North Carolina*, iv, p. xx; Weston, *Documents Connected with the History of South Carolina*, p. 82; Ellis and Evans, *History of Lancaster County, Pa.*, chs. iii, xxvi.

[6]Parkman, *Pontiac*, ii; Griffis, *Sir William Johnson*, p. 6; Simms' *Frontiersmen of New York*.

[7]Monette, *Mississippi Valley*, i, p. 311.

[8]*Wis. Hist. Colls.*, xi, p. 50; Hinsdale, *Old Northwest*, p. 121; Burke, "Oration on Conciliation," *Works* (1872 ed.), i, p. 473.

[9]Roosevelt, *Winning of the West*, and citations there given; Cutler's *Life of Cutler*.

[10]Scribner's *Statistical Atlas*, xxxviii, plate 13; McMaster, *Hist. of People of U.S.*, i, pp. 4, 60, 61; Imlay and Filson, *Western Territory of America* (London, 1793); Rochefoucault-Liancourt, *Travels Through the United States of North America* (London 1799); Michaux's "Journal," in *Proceedings American Philosophical Society*, xxv, No. 129; Forman, *Narrative of a Journey Down the Ohio and Mississippi in 1780–90* (Cincinnati, 1888); Bartram, *Travels Through North Carolina, etc.* (London, 1792); Pope, *Tour Through the Southern and Western Territories, etc.* (Richmond, 1792); Weld, *Travels Through the States of North America* (London, 1799); Baily, *Journal of a Tour in the Unsettled States of North America, 1796–7* (London, 1856); *Pennsylvania Magazine of History*, July, 1886; Winsor, *Narrative and Critical History of America*, vii, pp. 491, 492, citations.

[11]Scribner's *Statistical Atlas*, xxxix.

[12]Turner, *Character and Influence of the Indian Trade in Wisconsin* (Johns Hopkins University Studies, Series ix), pp. 61 ff.

[13]Monette, *History of the Mississippi Valley*, ii; Flint, *Travels and Residence in Mississippi*; Flint, *Geography and History of the Western States*; *Abridgment of Debates of Congress*, vii, pp. 397, 398, 404; Holmes, *Account of the U.S.*; Kingdom, *America and the British Colonies* (London, 1820); Grund, *Americans*, ii, chs. i, iii, vi (although writing in 1836, he treats of conditions that grew out of western advance from the era of 1820 to that time); Peck, *Guide for Emigrants* (Boston, 1831); Darby, *Emigrants' Guide to Western and Southwestern States and Territories*; Dana, *Geographical Sketches in the Western Country*; Kinzie, *Waubun*; Keating, *Narrative of Long's Expedition*; Schoolcraft, *Discovery of the Sources of the Mississippi River*, *Travels in the Central Portions of the Mississippi Valley*, and *Lead Mines of the Missouri*; Andreas, *History of Illinois*, i, 86–99; Hurlbut, *Chicago Antiquities*; McKenney, *Tour to the Lakes*.

[14]Darby, *Emigrants' Guide*, pp. 272 ff.; Benton, *Abridgment of Debates*, vii, p. 397.

[15]*DeBow's Review*, iv, p. 254; xvii, p. 428.

[16]Grund, *Americans*, ii, p. 8.

[17]Peck, *New Guide to the West* (Cincinnati, 1848), ch. iv; Parkman, *Oregon Trail*; Hall, *The West* (Cincinnati, 1848); Pierce, *Incidents of Western Travel*; Murray, *Travels in North America*; Lloyd, *Steamboat Directory* (Cincinnati, 1856); "Forty Days in a Western Hotel" (Chicago), in *Putnam's Magazine*, December, 1854; Mackay, *The Western World*, ii, ch. ii, iii; Meeker, *Life in the West*; Bogen, *German in America* (Boston, 1851); Olmstead, *Texas Journey*; Greeley, *Recollections of a Busy Life*; Schouler, *History of the United States*, v, 261–267; Peyton, *Over the Alleghanies and Across the Prairies* London, 1870); Loughborough, *The Pacific Telegraph and Railway* (St. Louis, 1849); Whitney, *Project for a Railroad to the Pacific* (New York, 1849); Peyton, *Suggestions on Railroad Communication with the Pacific, and the Trade of China and the Indian Islands*; Benton, *Highway to the Pacific* (a speech delivered in the U.S. Senate, December 16, 1850).

[18]A writer in *The Home Missionary* (1850), p. 239, reporting Wisconsin conditions, exclaims: "Think of this, people of the enlightened East. What an example, to come from the very frontiers of civilization!" But one of the missionaries writes: "In a few years Wisconsin will no longer be considered as the West, or as an outpost of civilization, any more than Western New York or the Western Reserve."

[19]H. H. Bancroft, *History of California, History of Oregon,* and *Popular Tribunals;* Shinn, *Mining Camps.*

[20]See the suggestive paper by Prof. Jesse Macy, *The Institutional Beginnings of a Western State.*

[21]Shinn, *Mining Camps.*

[22]Compare Thorpe, in *Annals American Academy of Political and Social Science,* September 1891; Bryce, *American Commonwealth* (1888), ii, p. 689.

[23]Loria, *Analisi della Proprieta Capitalista,* ii, p. 15.

[24]Compare *Observations on the North American Land Company* (London, 1796), pp. xv, 144; Logan, *History of Upper South Carolina,* i, pp. 149–151; Turner, *Character and Influence of the Indian Trade in Wisconsin,* p. 18; Peck, *New Guide for Emigrants* (Boston, 1837), ch. iv; *Compendium Eleventh Census,* i, p. xl.

[25]But Lewis and Clark were the first to explore the route from the Missouri to the Columbia.

[26]On the effect of the fur trade in opening the routes of migration, see the author's *Character and Influence of the Indian Trade in Wisconsin.*

[27]Lodge, *English Colonies,* p. 152 and citations; Logan, *Hist. of Upper South Carolina,* i, p. 151.

[28]Flint, *Recollections.* p. 9.

[29]See Monette, *Mississippi Valley,* i, p. 344.

[30]Coues's *Lewis and Clark's Expedition,* i, pp. 2, 253–259; Benton, in *Cong. Record,* xxiii, p. 57.

[31]Hehn, *Das Salz* (Berlin, 1873).

[32]*Col. Records of N.C.,* v, p. 3.

[33]Finley, *Hist. of the Insurrection of the Four Western Counties of Pennsylvania in the Year 1794* (Philadelphia, 1796), p. 35.

[34]Hale, *Daniel Boone,* etc., a pamphlet in the library of the State Historical Society of Wisconsin.

[35]Compare Baily, *Tour in the Unsettled Parts of North America* (London, 1856), pp. 217–219, where a similar analysis is made for 1796.

[36]"Spottswood Papers," in *Collections of Virginia Historical Society,* i, ii.

[37][Burke], *European Settlements,* etc. (1765 ed.), ii, p. 200.

[38]*Wis. Hist. Colls.,* xii, pp. 7 ff.

[39]Weston, *Documents Connected with History of South Carolina,* p. 61.

[40]See the admirable monograph by Prof. H. B. Adams, *Maryland's Influence on the Land Cessions;* and also Welling, in *Papers American Historical Association,* iii, p. 411.

[41]Adams's *Memoirs,* ix, pp. 247, 248.

[42]Author's article in *The Aegis,* November 8, 1892.

[43]*Political Science Quarterly,* ii, p. 457. Compare Sumner, *Alexander Hamilton,* chs. ii–vii.

[44]Compare Wilson, *Division and Reunion,* pp. 15, 24.

[45]On the relation of frontier conditions to Revolutionary taxation, see Sumner, *Alexander Hamilton,* ch. iii.

[46]I have refrained from dwelling on the lawless characteristics of the frontier, because they are sufficiently well known. The gambler and desperado, the regulators of the Carolinas and the vigilantes of California, are types of that line of scum that the waves of advancing civilization bore before them, and of the growth of spontaneous organs of authority where legal authority was absent. Compare Barrows, *United State of Yesterday and To-morrow;* Shinn, *Mining Camps;* and Bancroft, *Popular Tribunals.* The humor, bravery, and rude strength, as well as the vices of the frontier in its worst aspect, have left traces on American character, language, and literature, not soon to be effaced.

[47]*Debates in the Constitutional Convention,* 1829–1830.

[48][McCrady] *Eminent and Representative Men of the Carolinas,* i, p. 43.

[49]*Speech in the Senate,* March 1, 1825; *Register of Debates,* i, 721.

[50]*Plea for the West* (Cincinnati, 1835), pp. 11 ff.

[51]Colonial travellers agree in remarking on the phlegmatic characteristics of the colonists. It has frequently been asked how such a people could have developed that strained nervous energy now

characteristic of them. Compare Sumner, *Alexander Hamilton*, p. 98, and Adams's *History of the United States*, i, p. 60; ix, pp. 240, 241. The transition appears to become marked at the close of the War of 1812, a period when interest centered upon the development of the West, and the West was noted for restless energy. Grund, *Americans*, ii, ch. i.

CONTRIBUTORS

MARTIN RIDGE is Senior Research Associate at the Henry E. Huntington Library, San Marino, California—a position first held by Frederick Jackson Turner.

RAY ALLEN BILLINGTON (1903–1981) was one of the foremost scholars of the American West and the biographer of Frederick Jackson Turner.

JAMES P. DANKY is Newspapers and Periodicals Librarian at the State Historical Society of Wisconsin, Madison.

◆